JANE AUSTEN'S

Emma

EMMA. Contains material originally published in magazine form as EMMA #1-5. First printing 2011. ISBN# 978-0-7851-5685-7. Published by MARVEL WORLDWIDE, INC., a subsidiary of MARVEL ENTERTAINMENT, LLC. OFFICE OF PUBLICATION: 135 West 50th Street, New York, NY 10020. Copyright © 2011 Marvel Characters, Inc. All rights reserved. $19.99 per copy in the U.S. and $21.99 in Canada (GST #R127032852); Canadian Agreement #40668537. All characters featured in this issue and the distinctive names and likenesses thereof, and all related indicia are trademarks of Marvel Characters, Inc. No similarity between any of the names, characters, persons, and/or institutions in this magazine with those of any living or dead person or institution is intended, and any such similarity which may exist is purely coincidental. **Printed in the U.S.A.** ALAN FINE, EVP - Office of the President, Marvel Worldwide, Inc. and EVP & CMO Marvel Characters B.V.; DAN BUCKLEY, Publisher & President - Print, Animation & Digital Divisions; JOE QUESADA, Chief Creative Officer; JIM SOKOLOWSKI, Chief Operating Officer; DAVID BOGART, SVP of Business Affairs & Talent Management; TOM BREVOORT, SVP of Publishing; C.B. CEBULSKI, SVP of Creator & Content Development; DAVID GABRIEL, SVP of Publishing Sales & Circulation; MICHAEL PASCIULLO, SVP of Brand Planning & Communications; JIM O'KEEFE, VP of Operations & Logistics; DAN CARR, Executive Director of Publishing Technology; SUSAN CRESPI, Editorial Operations Manager; ALEX MORALES, Publishing Operations Manager; STAN LEE, Chairman Emeritus. For information regarding advertising in Marvel Comics or on Marvel.com, please contact John Dokes, SVP Integrated Sales and Marketing, at jdokes@marvel.com. For Marvel subscription inquiries, please call 800-217-9158. **Manufactured between 7/25/2011 and 8/22/2011** by R.R. DONNELLEY, INC., SALEM, VA, USA.

10 9 8 7 6 5 4 3 2 1

JANE AUSTEN'S Emma

Based on the novel by

Jane Austen

Writer	Nancy Butler
Artist	Janet K. Lee
Letterer	Nate Piekos
Production	Damien Lucchese, Irene Y. Lee, Mayela Gutierrez & Taylor Esposito
Editor	Sana Amanat
Senior Editor	Ralph Macchio

Collection Editor	Mark D. Beazley
Editorial Assistants	James Emmett & Joe Hochstein
Assistant Editors	Nelson Ribeiro & Alex Starbuck
Editor, Special Projects	Jennifer Grünwald
Senior Editor, Special Projects	Jeff Youngquist
Senior Vice President of Sales	David Gabriel
Book Design	Spring Hoteling

Editor in Chief	Axel Alonso
Chief Creative Officer	Joe Quesada
Publisher	Dan Buckley
Executive Producer	Alan Fine

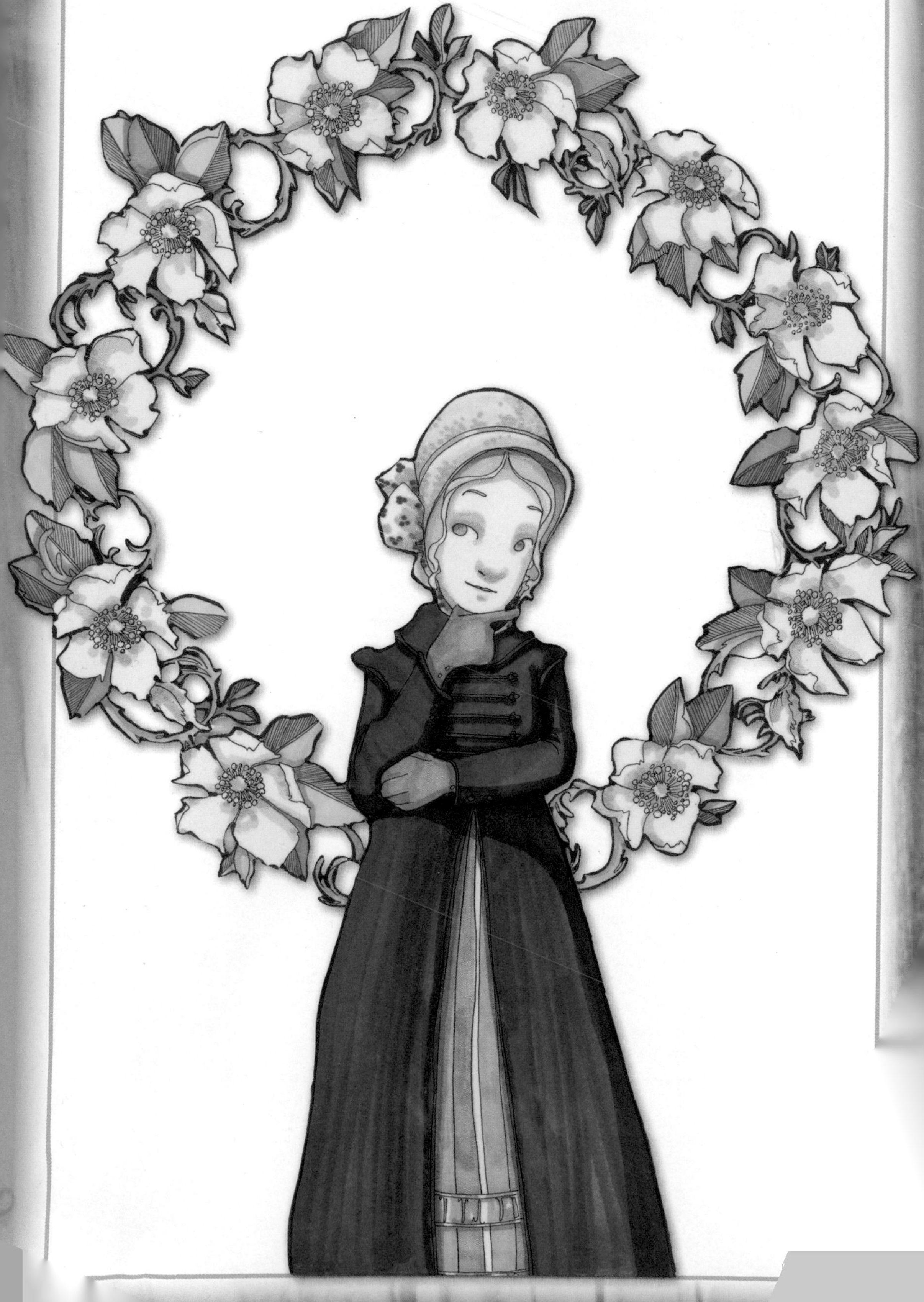

*E*mma is the third Austen adaptation I have done for Marvel, and once again an interviewer—this time a gentleman preparing a talk for the Jane Austen Society—asked me "What makes her work so timeless?" Of course, I trot out her biting social commentary and rapier wit as examples of why her books are still read and studied into this new century. But while working on this adaptation, I believe I discovered several other reasons for Jane's appeal to modern audiences.

Getting There is Half the Fun

The characters in this story seem obsessed by modes of transportation. Or more specifically, by people who have them and people who don't. Mr. Woodhouse, Emma's father, frets endlessly over the whims of his coachman and the perils to anyone traveling in bad weather; Emma brags about the good breeding of their cattle (carriage horses) and is not above calling for the coach to impress—or intimidate—a farmer's family; Mr. Elton, the vicar, lacking so much as a dogcart, hints around for lifts to parties on cold winter mornings; while local catch Frank Churchill careers around on a wild, black mare, scaring his stepmother to death. Mr. Knightley, so much the perfect gentlemen in all other respects, keeps no horses at his stately home, but is reduced to leasing them when required, much to Emma's mortification.

And then there is Mrs. Elton, the vicar's new bride, a wealthy, social-climbing harpy who promptly gifts her "caro sposo" with a carriage so that they can enter the village of Highbury in high style. But Mrs. Elton doesn't stop there . . . she constantly reminds anyone unlucky enough to be within earshot that her sister and brother-in-law possess not only a two-wheeled chaise, but an elegant, open-topped barouche-landau, which they use for exploring the countryside. There are odes to the barouche-landau in this story that could rival Keats.

So we see that during Austen's Regency, just as in modern times, the conferring of social status was often "all about the ride." Think of it this way: Mr. Woodhouse owned a staid, reliable Lincoln Town Car; Frank Churchill drove the muscle car; Mrs. Elton's relatives had the subcompact *and* the snazzy convertible Caddy; and Mr. Knightley, like Ferris Bueller, has to borrow transportation (but has oodles of charisma to make up for it).

Emmas Old and New

Then there is Emma herself, a heroine so contemporary she morphed seamlessly into Cher Horowitz in Amy Heckerling's 1995 film "Clueless." She is the consummate teen queen in both incarnations—preening, manipulative, a little ditzy in how she convinces herself that her woefully dense observations are spot on, falling rapidly into and out of love, and holding herself above the common fray all the while behaving as the most mortal of mortals.

But this privileged young woman is also a bird in a gilded cage, one who secretly chafes at the restrictions in her life—and make no mistake, our literary Emma is restricted. She rarely visits nearby London and prior to the story had never been to Box Hill, a scant seven miles from her home. Like many modern divas, her wealth is more of a barrier than a blessing.

Even Emma's romance is conducted with modern sensibilities. When a proposal comes at last from Mr. Knightley, it is not couched in the flowery language of the era, but utilizes such realistic phrases as "I cannot make speeches," "God knows I have been an indifferent lover," and "you hear nothing but truth from me." Hardly the stuff of maidenly dreams, but music to the ears of a brisk, discerning heroine.

No, Emma does not feel distant from us, not removed by several centuries from our own world. She feels like the heroine of a trendy chick lit novel or the hot new romantic comedy. It's as though Emma, both the book and the character, became Austen's ambassadors to the future, never syrupy or moralizing in that ponderous nineteenth-century way, but always tartly charming like the latest bistro cocktail.

Austen believed Emma was a character only her author could love, yet I think most readers love Emma, eventually—for her monstrous ego, not in spite of it. We simultaneously root for her to be humbled *and* happy . . . which is exactly what Austen gives us in the end.

Creating this adaptation of *Emma* was a challenge and a joy. One of the happier parts was working with illustrator Janet K. Lee, who found all the elegant beauty in the book and came up with some simply mouthwatering panels. I also want to thank my editor, Sana Amanat, and the rest of the Marvel team who kept ings moving ahead like a well-oiled machine. I hope you all, the Austen fans and the neophytes, have as much reading *Emma* as we had producing it

Emma Woodhouse, handsome, clever, and rich, had achieved nearly twenty-one years with very little to distress or vex her. She lived with her aged father and--after the marriage of her elder sister, Isabella--had been mistress of his house, Hartfield, for many years.

If there were any evils to Emma's situation, they were the power of having rather too much her own way and a disposition to think a little too well of herself. This danger was, at present, as yet unperceived...

The first ripple of disquiet occurred when Miss Taylor, Emma's beloved governess and companion of sixteen years, left Hartfield to marry a local landowner, *Mr. Weston*...

...Emma felt a gentle sorrow at the loss of Miss Taylor and knew she would miss her friend every hour of every day.

After supper that evening...

Poor Miss Taylor! I wish she were here again. What a pity it is that Mr. Weston ever thought of her!

You must not say that, Papa. Mr. Weston is such a good-humored, excellent man...and you know I encouraged the match. Would you have Miss Taylor remain with us forever, when she might have a house of her own?

This house is *three* times the size of *Randalls*.

Besides, Mr. Westons' estate lies only a little beyond Highbury. We shall always be visiting them and they us.

How am I to get so *far?* I could not walk half the distance to Randalls.

No, Papa, nobody thought of your walking. We must go in the carriage, to be sure.

What? Hmpph...James will not want to harness the horses to travel such a *little* way.

Have you forgotten? His daughter is now the Westons' housemaid. I assure you, James will always be willing to go to Randalls. In fact I doubt he will want to take us anywhere else.

Emma suggested a game of backgammon to distract her father, but their play was soon interrupted by a most welcome visitor...their neighbor *Mr. George Knightley*, brother to Isabella's husband and Emma's chief confidante.

Knightley, so kind of you to call on us at this late hour. But what a *shocking* walk you must have had.

Not at all. It is a beautiful moonlit night. And so mild, I must draw back from your great fire.

Ah, but you must have found it damp and dirty.

Dirty, sir? Just look at my boots. Not a *speck* on them.

By the by, I have not wished you joy. I hope the wedding went off tolerably well. I expect all the ladies cried.

Ah, poor Miss Taylor...

Say poor Mr. and Miss Woodhouse, if you please, but not poor Miss Taylor. I have a great regard for you and Emma, but when it comes to the question of dependence or independence--let me just say, it must be better to have only *one* to please than *two.*

Especially when one of them is such a fanciful troublesome creature.

Sadly, I confess I *am* sometimes troublesome...

Dearest Papa! I meant only myself. Mr. Knightly loves to find fault with *me,* you know--in a joking manner. We always say what we like to one another.

Emma knows I never flatter her. But I meant no reflection on anybody. Miss Taylor has had two people to see to; she will now have but one.

Emma bears everything so well, but I am sure she will miss her sorely.

It is impossible for Emma not to miss such a companion. But to see Miss Taylor settled and provided for in a home of her own...every friend of hers must be glad to see her so happily married.

You have forgotten one matter of joy to me--that I made the match myself. *And* I accomplished it after everyone said Mr. Weston would never marry again. But I determined that he should four years ago when we met him in the rain and Miss Taylor borrowed his umbrella.

When such success has blessed me, I cannot think I will leave off match-making.

Success? A straightforward man like Mr. Weston and a rational woman like Miss Taylor can surely be left to manage their own concerns.

Where is your merit in this, Emma?

Have you never known the triumph and pleasure of a lucky guess? If *I* had not encouraged Mr. Weston and smoothed many little matters it might have come to nothing at all.

I wager you are more likely to do *harm* than *good* by such interference.

Emma never thinks of herself, if she can do good to others.

But, pray, my dear, no more matches. They are silly things and break up one's family circle grievously.

Oh, I promise to make none for *myself*, Papa. But I must look about for a wife for *Mr. Elton*, our rector. He has been here a year and has fixed up his house so comfortably. It would be a shame for him to remain single any longer.

Elton is a deserving young man, to be sure, and I have a great regard for him myself. But if you want to be of service to him, ask him to dine.

Yes, Emma. That would be a much better thing. Ask him to dinner and help him to the best of the chicken and fish, but leave him to choose his own wife.

Depend upon it, a man of six and twenty can take care of himself.

Within the week, Emma and her father paid the Westons a wedding visit at Randalls.

Emma, there's some news I'd like to share with you. I...I'm not sure how much you know of Mr. Weston's first marriage.

I know he and his late wife had a son...*Frank Churchill*...whom no one in the village has met. Yet all of Highbury takes great pride in him. I've often wondered why he never visits here.

Mrs. Weston then proceeded to edify Emma.

"Mr. Weston was a captain in the militia when he wed Miss Churchill, who was from a wealthy family.

"They disapproved of the match and severed all ties with her.

"When his wife died, Mr. Weston could ill afford to care for a child.

"So Frank, whose birth had begun to heal the breach between the families, was raised by his mother's brother and his wife."

And took their name as his own.

Precisely. After Mr. Weston left the militia, he made a small fortune in trade and eventually purchased Randalls. He now visits Frank once a year in London and reports that he has grown into a charming and intelligent young man.

Alas, poor Frank is completely under the control of his aunt, who has no love for my husband.

So I gather we cannot expect a visit from young Mr. Churchill anytime soon.

Ah, but there you are wrong, my dear. Frank Churchill has written me a most handsome letter felicitating me on my marriage and promising to pay us a bridal visit in the near future.

That is happy news, indeed. All of Highbury will be awaiting his visit with the greatest anticipation.

And what of your sentiments, Emma?

I am always eager to encounter any young person who is...how did you describe him...? *Charming* and *intelligent*.

Mr. Woodhouse had a fondness for holding evening parties at Hartfield, and barely went a week by when the card tables were not set up.

His guests typically included the Westons, Mr. Knightley, Mr. Elton, and the Bates ladies-- an elderly widow and her spinster daughter who had rooms in Highbury.

This particular evening, he also included Mrs. Goddard, the mistress of the local boarding school.

Dear Emma, what a lively gathering you have arranged. Your father is certainly in his element, with friends all about him.

This is *Miss Harriet Smith*, who has recently come to board with me at the school.

...ss Woodhouse, I ...m so happy to make ...our acquaintance ...t last.

And if you will permit me, I would like to compliment you on your home. It is in **all ways** most superior in style to what I have been used to.

You are most welcome here, Miss Smith. It is always a pleasure to meet a new guest, especially one so close to my own age. I suspect we will discover any number of shared interests.

I do hope so.

Find you... seat at one... tables, my... will be a... directly...

I do know... wo...

Once Harriet had departed and settled next to Mr. Elton...

Harriet is the sweetest creature, neither shy nor unwilling to talk, yet not pushing or presumptuous in her manner.

Alas, she is **somebody's** daughter, if I may make so indelicate an observation. Her board is paid each month by a solicitor in London...and I leave you to draw your own conclusions.

Poor girl, to have no family of her own.

She was, until recently, staying with the Martins, who lease a farm from Mr. Knightley. They are well thought of in their parish--

But **coarse** and **unpolished** company for a girl of such attributes.

It would be a kindness to befriend her, Emma. She could learn a great deal from you.

Ah, I see your father is waving to me. I must go now and give him a proper greeting.

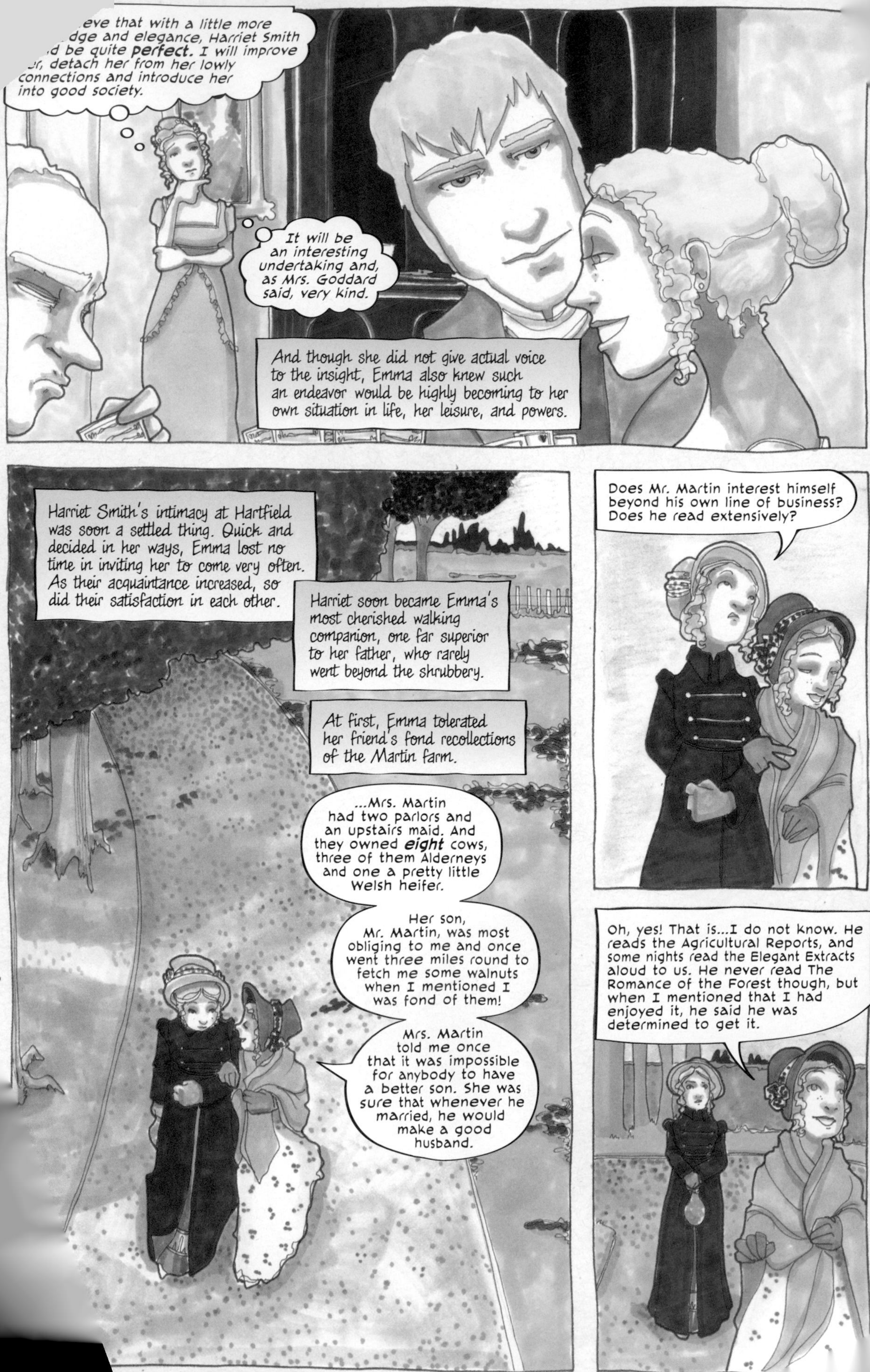
eve that with a little more dge and elegance, Harriet Smith d be quite **perfect.** I will improve r, detach her from her lowly connections and introduce her into good society.
It will be an interesting undertaking and, as Mrs. Goddard said, very kind.
And though she did not give actual voice to the insight, Emma also knew such an endeavor would be highly becoming to her own situation in life, her leisure, and powers.
Harriet Smith's intimacy at Hartfield was soon a settled thing. Quick and decided in her ways, Emma lost no time in inviting her to come very often. As their acquaintance increased, so did their satisfaction in each other.
Harriet soon became Emma's most cherished walking companion, one far superior to her father, who rarely went beyond the shrubbery.
At first, Emma tolerated her friend's fond recollections of the Martin farm.
...Mrs. Martin had two parlors and an upstairs maid. And they owned ***eight*** cows, three of them Alderneys and one a pretty little Welsh heifer.
Her son, Mr. Martin, was most obliging to me and once went three miles round to fetch me some walnuts when I mentioned I was fond of them!
Mrs. Martin told me once that it was impossible for anybody to have a better son. She was sure that whenever he married, he would make a good husband.
Does Mr. Martin interest himself beyond his own line of business? Does he read extensively?
Oh, yes! That is...I do not know. He reads the Agricultural Reports, and some nights read the Elegant Extracts aloud to us. He never read The Romance of the Forest though, but when I mentioned that I had enjoyed it, he said he was determined to get it.

"...hat does he look like? I am sure he has ridden past me any number of times in Highbury, but a farmer on horseback would do little to raise my curiosity."

"He is not handsome. I thought him plain at first, though I do not think him so now. One does not, you know, after a time."

"Harriet, I wish you may not get into a scrape, whenever he does marry. His sisters, from what you say, have been educated and are not altogether objectionable."

"But it does not follow that Mr. Martin will marry anybody fit for you to notice."

"The misfortune of your birth must make you particularly careful in your associates. There can be no doubt of your being a gentleman's daughter, and you must support your claim to that station with everything in your power."

"Else there are plenty who would take pleasure in degrading you."

"I suppose there are. Yet while I am with you at Hartfield, I am not afraid of what anyone can do."

"You understand the force of influence very well, Harriet. Yet I would have you so firmly established in good society to be independent even of Hartfield or Miss Woodhouse."

"To that end, it will be advisable to have as few odd acquaintances as possible. Don't let your fondness for his sisters draw you into friendship with his wife, who is likely to be an uneducated farm girl."

"I can't credit Mr. Martin would marry someone who had not been well brought up...though I do not mean to set up my opinion against yours."

"And I am sure I shall *not* wish for the acquaintance of Robert Martin's wife."

The two friends happened upon Mr. Martin the very next morning...

Halloa, Miss Smith, I give you good day!

Mr. Martin! G-good day to you, sir.

I...I did not think to see you this far from Highbury.

Miss Woodhouse and I have been visiting the Westons at Randalls.

After a brief exchange of pleasantries, the girls moved on.

Imagine meeting him by chance! He said he is rarely on this road.

So what do you think of him, Miss Woodhouse? Is he like what you expected?

He is very plain... remarkably plain. Though that is nothing compared to his want of gentility. I had no idea he could be so very *clownish.*

To be sure, he is not so refined as a true gentleman...

After being in the company of such gentlemen at Hartfield, you could hardly spend time with Mr. Martin now without perceiving him to be a very inferior creature.

I imagine you are wondering how you ever found him agreeable at all. Do you not begin to feel that now?

He is certainly unlike Mr. Knightley in his manner.

Mr. Knightley's air is so remarkably good, it's hardly fair to compare anyone to him. But how does Mr. Martin compare to, say, Mr. Weston or Mr. Elton?

Oh, yes. There is a great difference. Though Mr. Weston is quite old--

All the more rea[son to] cultivate good ma[nners.] They become incre[asingly] valuable as we ag[e. How] will Mr. Martin be [at] Mr. Weston's age? A gross, vulgar farmer, inattentive to his appearance, his thoughts only of profit.

Will he, indeed? That would be very bad.

He is already engrossed in his labor, just now spoke of little but the cattle market in Kingston, and did not even *remember* to look for your book.

I wonder he did not remember the book...

No, he has not the air of Knightley, the wisdom of Weston, nor yet, the gentle civility of Mr. Elton. That is perhaps the greatest of attributes. Any young man would do well to take Mr. Elton as a model.

It strikes me that Mr. Elton's gentleness has increased of late...as though there were *some* young lady whose notice he wished to engage. I can only think of one such lady who has come recently to our neighborhood.

Surely not *me*, Miss Woodhouse.

He told me last week that you *were*...well, I cannot repeat a compliment spoken in confidence, but I *can* assure you that it was the warmest personal praise.

I don't know what to say...except that I have always found Mr. Elton to be most agreeable.

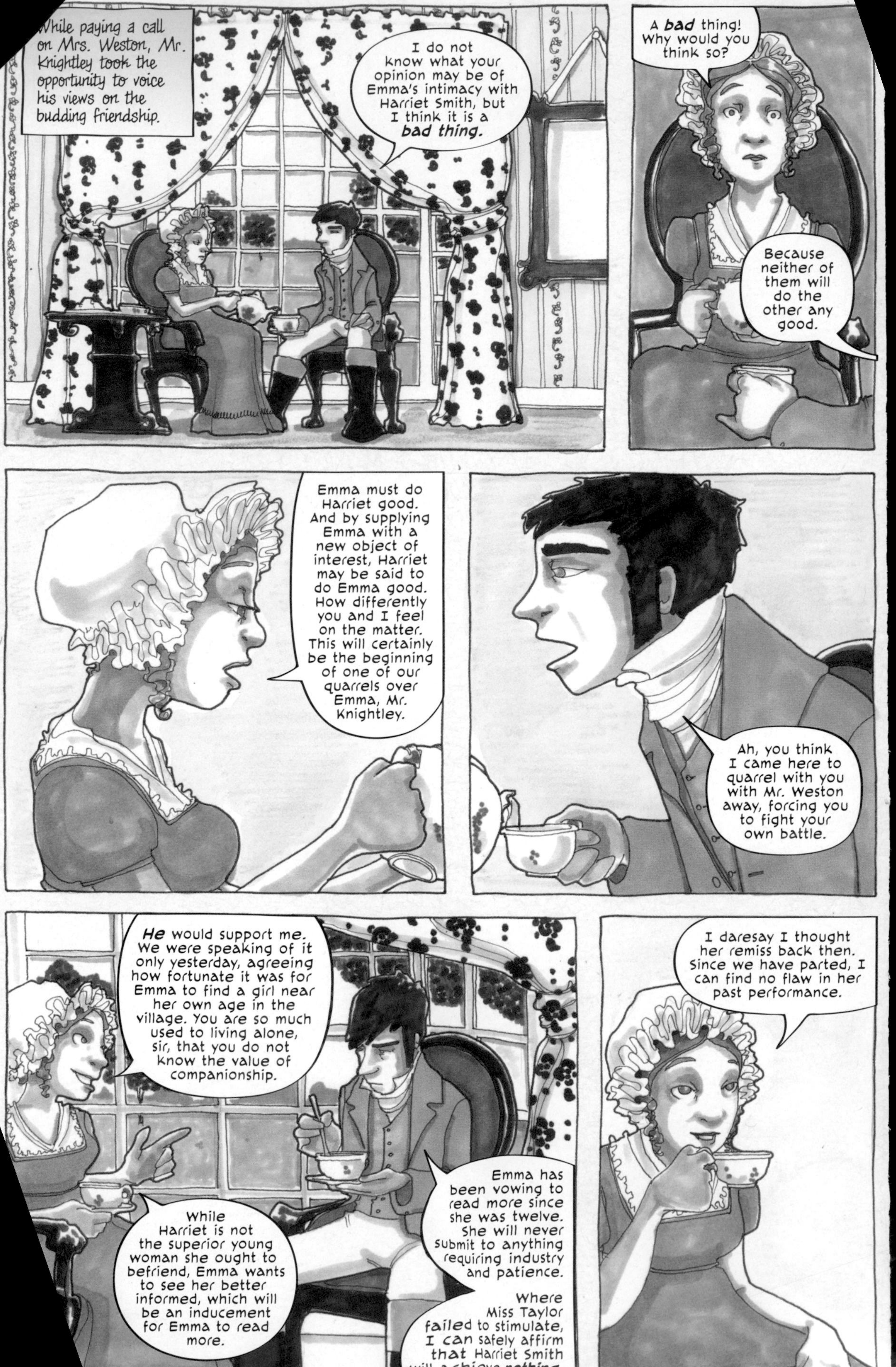
While paying a call on Mrs. Weston, Mr. Knightley took the opportunity to voice his views on the budding friendship.
I do not know what your opinion may be of Emma's intimacy with Harriet Smith, but I think it is a bad thing.
A bad thing! Why would you think so?
Because neither of them will do the other any good.
Emma must do Harriet good. And by supplying Emma with a new object of interest, Harriet may be said to do Emma good. How differently you and I feel on the matter. This will certainly be the beginning of one of our quarrels over Emma, Mr. Knightley.
Ah, you think I came here to quarrel with you with Mr. Weston away, forcing you to fight your own battle.
He would support me. We were speaking of it only yesterday, agreeing how fortunate it was for Emma to find a girl near her own age in the village. You are so much used to living alone, sir, that you do not know the value of companionship.
While Harriet is not the superior young woman she ought to befriend, Emma wants to see her better informed, which will be an inducement for Emma to read more.
Emma has been vowing to read more since she was twelve. She will never submit to anything requiring industry and patience.
Where Miss Taylor failed to stimulate, I can safely affirm that Harriet Smith will achieve nothing.
I daresay I thought her remiss back then. Since we have parted, I can find no flaw in her past performance.

I, fortunately, have had no such charm thrown over my senses. I see Emma as she is--spoiled by being the cleverest of her family.

And the matter is not helped by Harriet, who knows nothing herself and looks upon Emma as knowing everything.

She is a flatterer in all her ways, though not by design. How can Emma imagine she has anything to learn when Harriet presents such a delightful inferiority?

And as for Har[riet] she gain by the [ ] Hartfield will [ ] dissatisfied with [ ] places she belo[ngs] Emma's tutela[ge] grow just refine[d] be uncomfortable with those among whom birth and circumstances have placed her home.

I have more faith in Emma's good sense than you do-- or am more anxious for her present comfort, so I cannot lament the friendship.

And did not Emma look well last night?

Ah, you would rather speak of her person than her mind.

Very well, I will not attempt to deny that Emma is pretty. I've seldom seen a face or figure that is more pleasing. But I am a partial, old friend.

She is loveliness itself, is she not?

I love to look at her, and will add this praise: I do not believe she is personally vain. She is little occupied with her looks.

No, her vanity lies another way.

And so, Mrs. Weston, I am not to be talked out of my dislike for Harriet or of my dread of Emma's particular vanity doing them both harm.

And I remain stout in my confidence of its not doing them any harm. With all Emma's little faults, she is an excellent creature. Where she errs once, she is in the right a hundred times.

Perhaps I will bide my time and wait to discuss the matter with my brother and Isabella when they come to Hartfield for Christmas.

Oh, I pray you do not make Emma a source of public discussion. Her father approves the friendship--and it is to *him alone* she answers.

Besides, Mrs. John Knightley is easily alarmed and might worry over her sister.

I promise I will not raise an outcry. But I have a very sincere interest in Emma, much more than I ever felt for Isabella. There is a curiosity, almost an anxiety. I wonder what will become of her.

So do I. She says she will never marry.

Which means nothing at all. I doubt she has ever met a man she cared for. It would not be a bad thing for her to be very much in love with a proper object. I should like to see Emma in love, and in some doubt of a return; it would do her good.

But there is nobody hereabouts to attach her and she goes so seldom from home.

Yes...there does, indeed, seem little to tempt her to break her resolution at present.

One morning, near the end of November...

Miss Woodhouse, I'm most happy to see you. I so rarely catch you alone.

A pleasure, Mr. Elton.

I've finished my own errands and am waiting for Harriet. She has gone into the stationers for some charcoal sticks. I intend to begin instructing her in still life composition this afternoon.

Ah, you have given Miss Smith so much...all she required to make her graceful and easy. She was a beautiful creature when she came to you, but the attractions you have added are infinitely superior to those supplied by nature.

I am glad you think I have been useful to her. She really only needed drawing out. I have done very little.

If a gentleman might contradict a lady-- Skilful has been the hand...

Great has been the pleasure. In truth, I never met with a disposition more amiable.

What an exquisite possession a *portrait* of Harriet would be. I almost long to attempt her likeness myself. If Harriet would only sit for me, how delighted I should be!

It would indeed be a delight! Let me entreat you, Miss Woodhouse, to exercise so charming a talent in favor of your friend. How could you suppose me ignorant of your drawings? Is not Hartfield rich in specimens of your landscapes and flowers?

I wish he would save his raptures for Harriet's face, and not my drawings.

Well, if you give me such kind encouragement, Mr. Elton, I believe I shall try. Harriet's features are very delicate, which makes a likeness difficult.

Exactly so--the shape of the eye and the lines about the mouth--yet I have not a doubt of your success. Pray, pray attempt it.

And she thinks so little of her own beauty, I shall have to work to convince her.

I have observed her modesty myself. But I cannot imagine she will not allow herself to be persuaded by you.

When Harriet emerged from the shop and heard the proposal, she did resist...

Oh, dear! Sit for a portrait? I would *never* consider such a thing.

...but she had no scruples which could stand many minutes against the earnest pressing of both the others.

Once the three were back at Hartfield, Emma retrieved her portfolio of portraits so that Harriet might choose a style.

These are lovely. But...um, they all appear incomplete.

Perhaps they are merely studies for the finished works.

No, I'm afraid I was always eager to move on to a new medium or style before I had mastered the one I was engaged in.

Oh, but they are such spirited drawings. I admire them enormously.

Quite so. I can see the merit in every one of them. Ah, here is one of your brother-in-law, Mr. John Knightley.

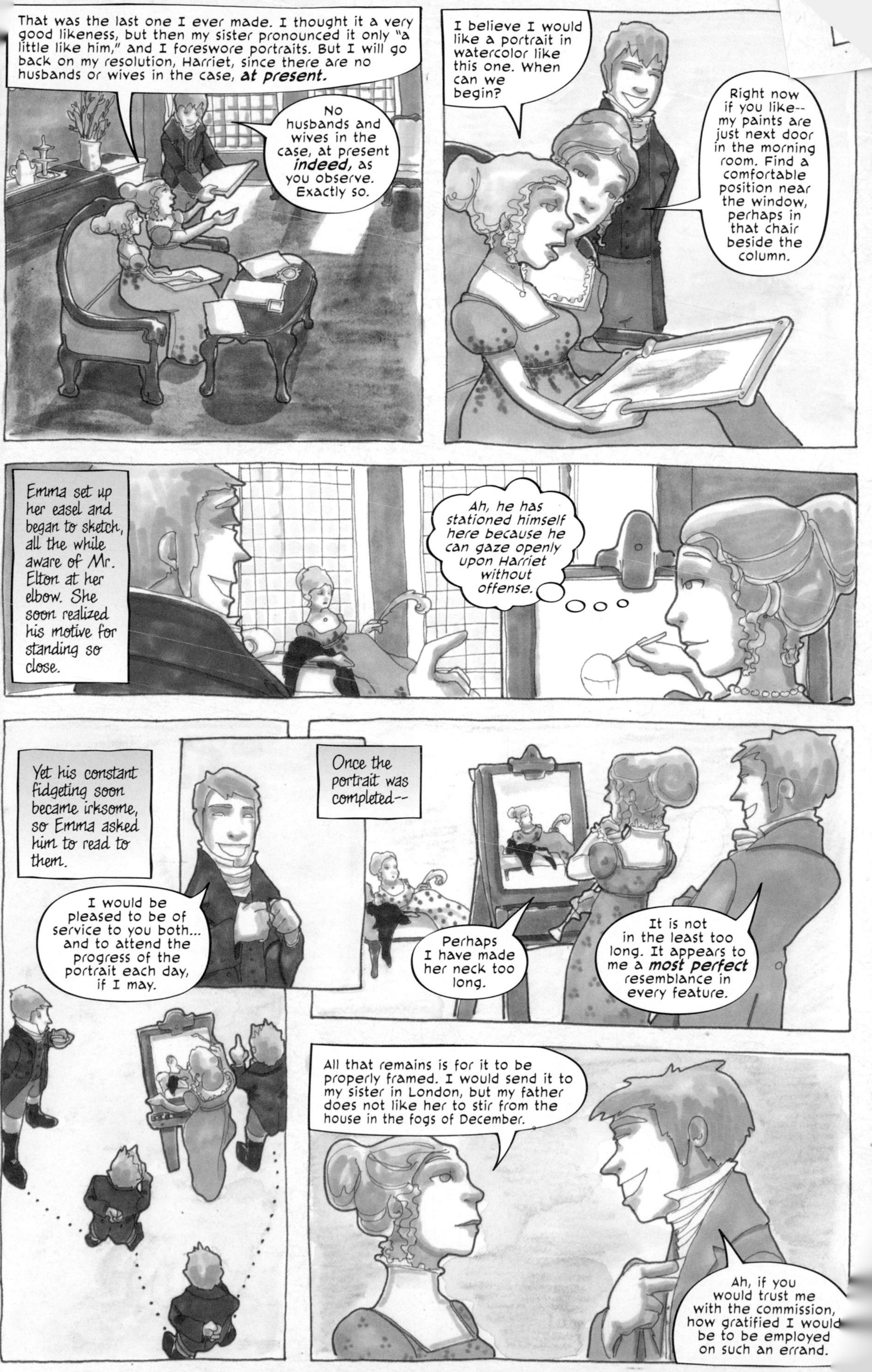

That was the last one I ever made. I thought it a very good likeness, but then my sister pronounced it only "a little like him," and I foreswore portraits. But I will go back on my resolution, Harriet, since there are no husbands or wives in the case, **at present.**
No husbands and wives in the case, at present ***indeed,*** as you observe. Exactly so.
I believe I would like a portrait in watercolor like this one. When can we begin?
Right now if you like-- my paints are just next door in the morning room. Find a comfortable position near the window, perhaps in that chair beside the column.
Emma set up her easel and began to sketch, all the while aware of Mr. Elton at her elbow. She soon realized his motive for standing so close.
Ah, he has stationed himself here because he can gaze openly upon Harriet without offense.
Yet his constant fidgeting soon became irksome, so Emma asked him to read to them.
I would be pleased to be of service to you both... and to attend the progress of the portrait each day, if I may.
Once the portrait was completed--
Perhaps I have made her neck too long.
It is not in the least too long. It appears to me a ***most perfect*** resemblance in every feature.
All that remains is for it to be properly framed. I would send it to my sister in London, but my father does not like her to stir from the house in the fogs of December.
Ah, if you would trust me with the commission, how gratified I would be to be employed on such an errand.

And so it was decided that Mr. Elton should carry the painting to London, choose the frame, and give the directions.

What a precious deposit.

The man is almost too gallant to be in love. But I suppose there are a hundred ways of being in love. He does sigh and languish more than I could endure... but he will suit Harriet exactly.

The next day, Harriet arrived at Hartfield for her usual morning visit, and left with a promise to return for dinner. She returned less than an hour later in a state of agitation.

Miss Woodhouse... oh my dear Miss Woodhouse!

Harriet! Whatever is the matter?

M-Mr. Martin went to Mrs. Goddard's this morning...to leave me a parcel from his sister Elizabeth. It was two songs I had lent her to copy. But in with the songs I found a note from Mr. Martin...

He has asked me to *marry* him, Miss Woodhouse! Who could have thought it? It was a good letter--at least I thought so--and he wrote as if he very much loved me.

You must read the letter and then tell me what I must do!

Emma scanned the note and found it very much above her expectation--expressing good sense, warm attachment, and delicacy of feeling, all in language both strong and unaffected.

Yes, it is a good letter. So good, that I suspect his sisters must have helped him. As for what you should do, you must answer it, and speedily.

But what should I say? You must advise me.

Oh, no. The response had much better be all your own. You will express yourself properly, I am sure. Such expressions of gratitude and concern for the pain you are causing him will spring unbidden to *your* mind.

Then you think I ought to *refuse* him?

My dear Harriet, are you in any *doubt* of that? I beg your pardon. I did not realize you needed my help regarding the intent of your letter; I imagined you were consulting me only on the wording of it.

I gather you mean to return a favorable answer.

I had no notion he liked me so much. Please... tell me what I ought to do.

I believe, as a general rule, that if a woman has *any* doubts about accepting a man, she should *refuse* him. If she hesitates to say "yes," then she ought to say "no."

But you must be the judge of your own happiness. If you prefer Mr. Martin to every man you have met, why hesitate?

Does anybody else occur to you under such a definition? Ah, Harriet, don't deceive yourself. Don't be run away with by gratitude and compassion. Of whom are you thinking at this moment?

I...I have now quite determined, really almost made up my mind...to *refuse* Mr. Martin.

Dear Harriet, you are doing just what you ought. I give myself joy of this. It would have grieved me to lose your acquaintance, which would have been the consequence of marrying him.

I could not have visited Mrs. Martin of Abbey-Mill Farm. Now I am secure of you forever.

Not have visited me! I never thought of that. It would have been too dreadful. What an escape!

And I could not have borne seeing you confined to the society of the illiterate and the vulgar. So we shall not be parted, my sweet, affectionate friend.

And so, with Emma's aid, the letter was written, sealed and sent. Harriet was safe, and although her spirits remained low that evening, Emma thought of one subject sure to brighten them.

Mr. Elton writes from London that he will be bringing your picture to Bond Street tomorrow...but for tonight, it is his companion, his solace, and his delight.

I am sure he has shown it to his mother and sisters, opening his designs to all his family.

Mr. Knightley called on Emma the next morning and soon turned the conversation to Harriet.

I must admit you have improved her, Emma. You have cured her of her schoolgirl giggle, for one thing.

Her character depends upon those she is with, but in good hands she will turn out a valuable woman.

Err...you say you are expecting her this morning?

At almost any moment.

Maybe she has been delayed. By a *visitor*, perhaps.

By Highbury gossips, you mean? Tiresome wretches.

Harriet may not consider everybody tiresome that you would.

I must tell you that I have reason to believe she will soon hear of something to her very great *advantage.*

Indeed, how so? Are you speaking of one who loves her? Who makes *you* their confidant?

I have it on good authority that Harriet Smith will soon receive an offer of marriage from Mr. Martin. He came to the Abbey two nights ago to consult me about it. He considers me a good friend and came to ask me whether I thought him imprudent for wanting to settle so early and whether I thought her too young.

I was very pleased by all that he said regarding his circumstances and plans. He is an excellent young man and I had no hesitation in advising him to marry.

So if he did not ask her yesterday, it is not unlikely that he is at Mrs. Goddard's today for that same purpose...and that Harriet will be detained by a visitor and not think him a tiresome wretch.

I will tell you something in return for what you told me. He did speak yesterday, that is, he wrote-- and was *refused.*

Then she is a greater *simpleton* than I ever believed her! What is the foolish girl about?!

It is always incomprehensible to a man that a woman should refuse an offer of marriage. Yet she did refuse him...I saw her answer.

Saw it! Yes, and *wrote* it too, I wager! This is your doing, Emma. You persuaded her to refuse him!

And if I did, I should not feel that I had done wrong. Mr. Martin is not Harriet's equal and I am surprised he should have ventured to address her.

Not Harriet's *equal!* He is as much her *superior* in sense as in situation. Emma, your infatuation about that girl *blinds* you.

She is the natural daughter of nobody knows whom, with probably no settled provision, and certainly no respectable relations. She is pretty and good-tempered, and that is *all.*

I nearly advised Martin against her, but there is no reasoning with a man in love.

It also crossed my mind that you would not mind seeing your friend settled and that with all your partiality for Harriet you would think it a *good* match.

How could you know so little of me? That I would think a *farmer* a good match for my intimate friend? The sphere in which she moves is much above his. It would be a degradation.

A degradation to illegitimacy and ignorance, to be married to a respectable, intelligent gentleman-farmer!

There can scarcely be a doubt that her father is a gentleman of fortune--her allowance is very liberal; nothing has ever been grudged for her improvement or comfort.

Furthermore, I know that Harriet is *exactly* what every man delights in--what at once bewitches his senses and satisfies his judgment. Were you, yourself, ever to marry, she is the very woman for *you.* And so I say again she is superior to Robert Martin.

She was happy with the Martins this summer. She had no sense of superiority then. If she has it now, you have given it.

Martin would never have proceeded if he thought her disinclined to him. Depend on it he had encouragement.

You have been no *friend* to Harriet Smith, Emma, puffing her up. Vanity working on a weak head produces every sort of *mischief.*

It is clear we think very differently on this point, Mr. Knightley. We shall only be making each other more angry if we continue.

I will say only this... knowing your love of matchmaking, it is fair to assume you have *other* plans for Harriet, and as a friend I must hint to you that if *Elton* is the man, think your labor in *vain.*

You are quite wrong about my plans.

Elton is not likely to throw himself away by making an imprudent match. He may talk sentimentally, but he will act rationally. I've often heard him speak with animation of his sisters' friends, a family of young ladies with twenty thousand pounds apiece.

I am obliged to you, and if I had my heart set on Mr. Elton marrying Harriet, it would have been kind of you to open my eyes.

But at present I only want to keep Harriet to myself.

I have *done* with matchmaking indeed.

Then I will bid you good morning.

Knightley left, still vexed, still feeling the young man's disappointment.

Emma also remained in a state of vexation. While she did not always feel so entirely convinced that her arguments were right and her adversary's wrong--as Mr. Knightley did-- she was certain she had done very well by Harriet.

Mr. Knightley was so much displeased by his quarrel with Emma that it was some time before he came again to visit her at Hartfield.

When he and Emma did meet, his dark looks showed she was not forgiven.

But Emma could not repent. On the contrary, her matchmaking plans were more and more justified by the events of the following days.

Harriet's portrait arrived from the framer in London that afternoon, and Mr. Elton came to see it the following morning, while Emma and Harriet were occupied with their latest pursuit-- the collecting of *riddles.*

It arrived only yesterday and when we unwrapped it, Papa insisted we place it above the mantel.

Ah, the wisdom and well-honed judgment of a parent.

Rather the doting tolerance of a fond father.

Not at all; it is a masterpiece of *delicacy* and *taste.*

Oh, but I have interrupted you and *Miss Smith*--

We are transcribing riddles into a book I made for Harriet. Perhaps you would care to write one for us.

I have never written, hardly ever, anything of the kind in my life. I fear not even Miss Woodhouse... or Miss Smith could inspire me.

But the next morning, Mr. Elton called to drop off a note...a charade, he said, written by a friend in honor of a lady he admired.

Being my friend's, I do not offer it for Miss Smith's collection, but perhaps *you* might not dislike looking at it.

And then he quickly departed.

Take it, Harriet, it is for you.

I am all a'tremor.

Very well, I shall read it.

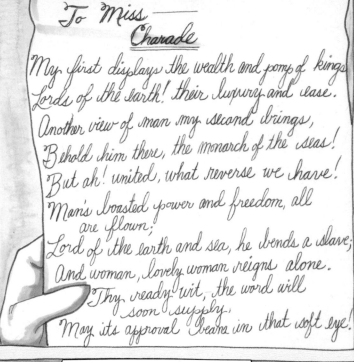

To Miss ——

Charade

My first displays the wealth and pomp of kings
Lords of the earth! their luxury and ease.
Another view of man my second brings,
Behold him there, the monarch of the seas!
But ah! united, what reverse we have!
Man's boasted power and freedom, all are flown;
Lord of the earth and sea, he bends a slave;
And woman, lovely woman reigns alone.
Thy ready wit, the word will soon supply,
May its approval beam in that soft eye!

Ah...*courtship.* I give you credit, Mr. Elton. This is very plainly saying "Miss Smith, please give me leave to court you."

Mr. Knightley, I wish you had the benefit of this. It would convince you, and for once in your life you would be obliged to admit yourself mistaken.

What can it mean, Miss Woodhouse? I have no idea. Does it speak of *Neptune, mermaids* and *sharks?* Who was the young man that wrote it?

Mermaids and sharks! My dear Harriet, the first two stanzas speak of the pomp of kings--court; the second two, of man upon the high seas--ship. And there can be no doubt it was written for you.

Courtship? From Mr. Elton? Oh, Miss Woodhouse...

I now have no doubt of his intentions. You are his object and will soon receive the *completest* proof of it. It is a sort of prologue to the play, a motto to the chapter.

How nicely you talk; I love to hear it. You and Mr. Elton are one as clever as the other.

Though it was now December, the weather was mild, and so the girls decided to pay a charitable visit to a needy family beyond the village.

As they passed Mr. Elton's vicarage...

Oh, what a sweet house. Such pretty yellow curtains...

You have never been inside? How I wish it could be contrived. But I cannot think of any tolerable pretense for going in.

I do wonder, Miss Woodhouse, that you should not be married. So charming as you are...

My being *charming* is not quite enough to induce me to marry; I must find the other person charming.

And, in truth, I have no intention of marrying.

I must see somebody far *superior* to anyone I have yet seen, to be tempted. And I would rather not be tempted.

I cannot easily change for the better, and if I were to marry, I must expect to repent it.

Dear me! It is odd to hear a woman talk so!

I have none of the inducements other women have to wed. Were I to fall in *love*, it would be a different matter. But I have never been in love. It is not my way or my nature.

I should be a fool to change my situation... I do not want for fortune, employment or consequence.

Never could I expect to be so truly beloved and important; so always first and always right in any man's eyes as I am in my father's.

But to become an *old maid*, like poor Miss Bates?

A formidable image, indeed! If I thought I should ever end up like Miss Bates...so silly--so prosy-- so undistinguished and unfastidious...I would marry tomorrow.

Though, to be fair, her poverty has not narrowed her mind, and if she had only a shilling to her name, she would give away half of it.

But how shall you occupy your time when you grow old?

Do you know Miss Bates' niece, Jane Fairfax?

As they entered the rough cottage, all idle topics were superseded.

Mine is an active, busy mind, and I don't know why I should be more in want of employment at fifty-one than I am at twenty-one. I will be very well off with my sister's children close by.

Oh, yes. We are forced into company together whenever she comes to Highbury. Heaven forbid I should *bore* people as Miss Bates does with tales of her niece--until one is quite sick of the name *Jane Fairfax.* I wish her very well, but she tires me to death.

Miss Woodhouse, how kind a' you and your friend t' look in on us an' all.

Emma was very compassionate, and the poor were as sure of relief from her person as from her purse. She could allow for their ignorance and had few romantic expectations of extraordinary virtue from those of little education. She entered into their troubles with ready sympathy, offering assistance with both good will and intelligence.

These are the sights, Harriet, to do one good. How trifling they make every thing else appear--I feel now as if I could think of *nothing* but these poor creatures all the rest of the day; and yet, who can say how soon it may all vanish from my mind?

Very true. Poor creatures! One can think of nothing else.

And really, I do not think the impression will soon be over. I do not think it will.

Oh! dear, no.

A bit farther down the lane, the girls came upon Mr. Elton-- intent upon the same errand.

Ah, I perceive you have just quitted the Hudspeth cottage. I was on my way there, but will now defer my visit until tomorrow and walk with you back toward Highbury.

To fall in with each other on such an errand as this, to meet in a charitable scheme...this will bring a great increase of love on each side. I should not wonder if it were to bring on the declaration. It **must**, if I were not here.

The ailing was resti more comfortably when we left-- Ah, but look--my bootlace is frayed. Why don't you two walk on?--and I will catch up once I have repaired it.

The couple set out together and Emma tried to hang back, but Mr. Elton and Harriet were never quite out of earshot. Emma was pleased to hear great animation in the vicar's voice, while Harriet listened with pleasing attention.

Mr. Elton soon caught sight of Emma and beckoned her to join them.

I'm sorry to be such a troublesome companion, but part of my lace is gone. Might we stop at your home, Mr. Elton, for a piece of twine or string?

I would be most happy to oblige you.

Once at the vicarage, Emma purposely engaged the housekeeper in conversation, leaving the erstwhile lovers alone in the parlor.

And this fine desk is where I write my sermons. It was a gift from Miss Woodhouse and her father.

Miss Woodhouse is the soul of generosity...

After some ten minutes of hearing herself lauded from afar, Emma felt obliged to make an appearance.

What a favorable aspect! Perhaps I **have** schemed successfully.

I must confess, I saw you go by from this window and determined to follow you.

And we are both pleased that you did.

But aside from some little gallantries, Mr. Elton did nothing to further his suit.

Cautious, very cautious. He advances inch by inch and will hazard nothing until he believes himself secure. Still, I flatter myself that this has been the occasion of much enjoyment to both and must be leading them forward to the great event.

The Christmas season brought with it the arrival of Emma's sister, Isabella, her husband, John Knightley and their children. Emma put aside her matchmaking schemes, and the visit became her prime object of interest.

There has been a sad change to Hartfield since last you were here. Poor Miss Taylor...it is a grievous business.

Oh, yes! A sad change, indeed. How you and Emma must miss her. I do hope she is well.

I trust there are no doubts about the air at Randalls.

None at all, John. I have never seen Mrs. Weston looking so well. Papa is only speaking of his own regrets.

...hn, unlike his brother, George Knightley, ...not a favorite of Emma's. His slights ...Isabella she could have borne, but not ...ccasional to her father.

And do you see her, sir, tolerably often?

Not near so often as I could wish.

Oh, Papa, we have missed seeing them only *one* entire day since they married. We have seen Mrs. or Mr. Weston--or both-- either here or at Randalls.

Just as it should be. I have always been telling you, Isabella, that the changes to Hartfield were not so material as you feared. And now after hearing Emma's account, I hope you are satisfied.

It's true she comes to visit, but then she always goes away again.

It would be hard on Mr. Weston if she did not. I will take the husband's part in this; *his* claims strike me with literal force.

As for Isabella, she has been married long enough to see the convenience of putting all the Mr. Westons aside.

Me, my love? Nobody is a *greater* advocate of matrimony than I am. I think Miss Taylor the most fortunate of women.

And as for slighting, that most excellent Mr. Weston... there is nothing he does not deserve.

Where is his son, Frank Churchill? Has the young man been here or not?

There was an expectation of his coming soon after the marriage, but it ended in nothing.

Emma wrote that he had sent a most handsome note to Mrs. Weston. I have no doubt he is an amiable young man. And how sad that he was not able to live at home with his father. There is something so shocking in a child being taken away from his parent.

My love, you need not imagine Mr. Weston felt what you would feel in giving up our own sons. Weston is an easy, cheerful man, but *not* one of strong feelings. He takes enjoyment more from his comforts than from family affection.

Emma could not like this reflection on Mr. Weston and had half a mind to take it up, but she struggled and let it pass.

Mr. Knightley was to dine with them that day, at first against the inclination of Mr. Woodhouse, who misliked sharing Isabella. But Emma prevailed upon her father, thinking it was time she made up with Knightley.

You have caught me at one of my favorite tasks... distracting my youngest niece and namesake.

Here, give me that rosy urchin...Ach, how delightfully plump she is and how tender.

She isn't a pullet, Mr. Knightley!

But what a *comfort* it is that we think alike about our nieces and nephews. Our opinions may differ about *men* and *women*, but with regard to these children, we never disagree.

Were you as little guided by whim and fancy in your dealings with men and women as you are with these children, we might always think alike.

To be sure, our discord must always arise from *my* being in the wrong.

I have the advantage of you by sixteen years and by not being a pretty young woman.

Come, dear Emma, let us be friends and say no more about it. Tell your aunt, little Emma, to set you a better example than to be renewing old grievances.

Yes, little Emma, grow up a better woman than your aunt. Be infinitely cleverer and not half so conceited.

Now, Mr. Knightley, admit that as far as good intentions go we were *both* in the right and assure me that Mr. Martin is not very disappointed.

A man cannot be more so.

Ah! I am very sorry. Yet, come, shake hands with me and let us be as we were.

Dinner was a quiet affair, and afterward the company gathered for a comfortable talk. As was usual with Mr. Woodhouse, the conversation soon turned to physicians.

It was an awkward business, your Mr. Wingfield sending you all to South End for the fall. We missed having you here.

Mr. Wingfield most *strenuously* recommended it, particularly for the weakness in little Bella's throat--both the sea air and bathing.

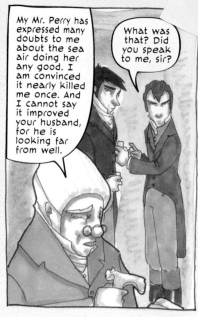

My Mr. Perry has expressed many doubts to me about the sea air doing her any good. I am convinced it nearly killed me once. And I cannot say it improved your husband, for he is looking far from well.

What was that? Did you speak to me, sir?

My father does not think you look well. I could have wished that you heeded me and saw Mr. Wingfield before we left London.

My dear Isabella, do not concern yourself with my looks. Be satisfied with doctoring and coddling yourself and your children...and let *me* look as I choose.

Mr. Knightley, I understand from your brother that your friend Mr. Graham is to engage a bailiff from Scotland. What will it answer?

And so Emma successfully drew John's attention from her sister.

But the evening did not end without the return of agitation.

You should have chosen Cromer over South End, Isabella. Mr. Perry advised against South End, saying you should rather have stayed in London than travel forty miles for bad air.

Mr. Perry would do very well to keep his opinion till it is asked for. I want his directions no more than his drugs. If *he* could tell me how to convey a family of seven a hundred miles at the cost of going forty--

True, true, it is a valid consideration.

And now, John, have I told you of my plans for moving the path to Langham away from the home meadow? We can drive there tomorrow and you shall tell me what you think.

The Westons were to hold a party on Christmas Eve, but Harriet came down with a fever the day before the event. Emma went to see her the next morning and was just leaving Mrs. Goddard's when she met Mr. Elton walking with John Knightley and his two boys.

Miss Woodhouse... what brings you out on such a frigid morning?

It's poor Harriet. I have just been paying a sick call on her. I'm afraid her throat is quite inflamed.

Dear me. I hope it does not turn putrid or infectious. She should send for Perry, for I hear there is influenza going around.

I am sure Mrs. Goddard will look after her properly. I only wish it was not so cold. If tonight's party were not such a special occasion, I would dissuade my father from going.

But, upon my word, Mr. Elton, *you* could certainly excuse yourself. You sound a bit hoarse already.

I...I am very gratified by your kind attention and your sweet concern, but I feel no inclination to give up the evening's entertainment. In fact, I shall look forward to seeing *you* there.

And if the cold is such an issue, rector, my wife and I would be happy to offer you a seat in our carriage.

After Mr. Elton moved on, John turned to Emma with a frown.

I never saw a man more intent on being agreeable than Mr. Elton. With men he can be rational but when he has *ladies* to please, every feature works.

Mr. Elton's manners are not perfect, but there is such perfect good will in him as one cannot but value.

He seems to have a great deal of good will toward you. I might even say he has made you his object of *affection.*

Me! Mr. Elton in love with *me?* What an idea! You are certainly imagining this.

Such imaginings have come to pass. And if it never occurred to you before, you should take it into consideration now and regulate your behavior accordingly. I speak as a friend, Emma--your manner to him is encouraging.

Thank you, but you are quite mistaken. We are good friends and *nothing* more.

Emma had quickly put John Knightley's words from her mind, but they rose again to haunt her at the Weston's party, when Mr. Elton noticeably singled her out for his attentions.

I spoke to Mrs. Goddard just before I returned home to dress. She said the patient was rather worse. I was saddened to hear it, hoping that your visit would have had the effect of a cordial on her.

Not even I can charm away a sore throat, Mr. Elton. Though her absence is a loss to our party.

Exactly so! She will be missed at every moment.

Emma was relieved when her brother-in-law drew her aside--until she comprehended the reason for the tete-a-tete.

A man must have a very good opinion of himself when he asks people to leave their own fireside on such a night. The absurdity of it--it is actually snowing!

The folly of not allowing others to be comfortable at home and the folly of people's not staying home and being comfortable when they can!

Emma found herself seated beside Mr. Weston at dinner and was content to listen to him speak of his son.

We lack only two guests to make up the right numbers--my Frank and your Miss Smith. I don't know if you heard me telling the others but we expect a visit from Frank in January.

What a great pleasure it will be to you! Mrs. Weston is so anxious to be acquainted with him that she must be as delighted as you are.

She fears his visit will be put off again...but I happen to know his obligations to attend his aunt next month will be postponed, so he should be here within a fortnight.

As her host related his son's many trials with his adoptive family, Emma found her compassion for his situation turning to admiration for his endurance.

Although I have vowed never to marry, there is something in the name, the idea of Frank Churchill, that has always interested me. And I believe that were I ever to wed, he would be the very person to suit me.

Not long after tea was served, Mr. John Knightley came into the drawing room with a dire announcement.

I have been surveying the weather and am sorry to report that the ground is covered with snow.

This will prove a *spirited* beginning to your winter sport, Mr. Woodhouse-- your coachman and horses making their way through a storm of snow.

What is to be *done*, Emma? What is to be done?

James will see us home safely, Papa. He is a skilled coachman and we have excellent horses.

You are all welcome to overnight here at Randalls. I am sure accommodations can be found.

Yes, I promise you will all be quite comfortable.

I cannot be away from Hartfield; my other *children* are there!

I shall walk if I have to and change my shoes the moment I get home. It is not the sort of thing that gives me a cold.

That would be most extraordinary, for in general *everything* gives you a cold.

I have just been down the drive to the main road and have also spoken with the coachmen.

There is but a dusting of snow beyond the grounds and the coachmen agree that there is nothing to fear if you leave now, or even an hour hence.

The carriages were immediately called for, and in the hubbub of her entire family piling into the Woodhouse coach, Emma found herself relegated to her brother-in-law's vehicle--alone with Mr. Elton.

Unnerved by John Knightley's earlier insinuations-- and her suspicions that Mr. Elton had drunk too much of Mr. Weston's good wine--Emma determined to speak with great calmness of the weather.

This is the harshest night I can recall--

Miss Woodhouse... I can restrain myself *no longer* and must take advantage of this *precious* opportunity...

...to tell you of sentiments that must already be long known to you...

...of my hopes and fears... of my willingness to *die* should you refuse me!

Mr. Elton! You will stop this instant!

Nay, I cannot!

I flatter myself that my ardent attachment, that my unexampled *passion* shall not fail to sway you!

Do you mistake me for my friend? I will happily deliver any message to her, but please...no more of this to me.

A message to *Miss Smith?* I never thought of Miss Smith in my whole life, never paid her any attention except as your friend! If she has fancied otherwise, her own wishes have misled her.

Who can think of Miss Smith when Miss *Woodhouse* is near? No, there is no unsteadiness of character; I have thought only of you.

Everything I have done or said has been with the object of marking my adoration of you. Can you doubt it? No, I am sure you have seen and understood me.

Not a bit, sir. So far from having long understood you, I have been in complete error with respect to your views. I am very sorry you gave way to your feelings. Nothing could be *further* from my wishes.

I rejoiced in your pursuit of my friend, and yet you claim you had no interest in her.

Miss Smith is a good sort of girl. There are some men who might not object to--Everybody has their *level*...

...But *I* do not so totally despair of an equal alliance as to be addressing Harriet Smith. No, my visits to Hartfield were for yourself alone, and for the encouragement I received.

Encouragement! Sir, you have been entirely mistaken. I saw you only as the admirer of my friend, else you could have been no more to me than a common acquaintance.

It is well that the mistake ends here, before Miss Smith became aware of the...great inequality that so troubles you.

I am sorry for your disappointment, but I have no thoughts of matrimony at present.

Mr. Elton was too angry to speak, and so they spent the balance of the journey in mutually mortified silence, until the carriage reached Vicarage Lane and Mr. Elton was out before another syllable passed.

Oh, how could I have been so mistaken? If only I had not persuaded Harriet into liking the man, I could have borne twice his presumption toward me.

How did this happen? Did I take up a false notion and bend everything to it?

But what of his eagerness over her portrait? Or the charade? Oh, and a *hundred* other things? How clearly they all pointed to Harriet.

Mr. Knightley warned me that Elton would never marry indiscreetly, and I scoffed at him.

Now it appears Mr. Knightley had a much truer knowledge of his character than I did. Mr. Elton is proving himself the opposite of all I believed--proud, assuming, and little concerned with the feelings of others.

I am also indebted to John for hinting at Elton's intentions, else I should have swooned tonight from pure shock.

As for Mr. Elton, I suppose he raised his eyes to me simply because he desired to marry well, and so I need not trouble to pity him.

Nearly a week passed before Emma could face the daunting task of revealing the truth to Harriet. Fortunately, she received some reassuring news the morning she was to confess to her friend.

Mr. Elton writes that he has gone to Bath for several weeks at the entreaty of some friends.

Do you not think it ill-judged of him to leave us in such an abrupt manner?

This is a most agreeable surprise. His absence just at this time is the very thing to be desired, and I commend him on having contrived it.

Yet when he returns, we **must** encounter each other. We three are fixed-- absolutely fixed--in the same place.

But we shall rely on indifference to cool misplaced ardor...

...and make the best of it.

Emma arrived at Mrs. Goddard's to find Harriet's health much improved.

I'm so pleased your cold is nearly gone. And I pray that what I am about to say does not send you into a relapse.

What could **you** ever say to cause me discomfort?

It...it appears I was wrong about Mr. Elton's affections. I misread his desire to be in company with **us** as a preference for **you.**

He...he proposed to me on the way home from the Westons' party-- Oh, to be sure, I **refused** him. But, dear Harriet, I am so sorry to have led you into such false hopes.

I am so ashamed. I was wrong and foolish to encourage you so actively...I vow I shall **never** be in charity with myself again.

I don't b-blame y-you. Indeed, I don't. I never truly believed a man of such distinction would look at me with affection. I could never have deserved him.

Only so kind and partial a friend as you would have thought it possible.

Nonsense! You are too modest by far. Now rest easy, and tomorrow you shall come for a stay at Hartfield. Furthermore, we shall have no specter of Mr. Elton to trouble us, for he has lately gone to Bath.

Emma then left her friend, convinced that in artlessness and simplicity of nature Harriet was the superior creature of the two.

Frank Churchill did not come to Randalls. When the proposed time in January drew near, Mrs. Weston received another note of excuse. Emma was the first to announce the news to Mr. Knightley.

The Churchills are likely at fault, though I daresay he might come if he really wanted to. I can't conceive that a man of twenty-three should not have liberty of mind or limb. Yet he sits still when he ought to move and instead writes flourishing letters full of falsehoods to Mrs. Weston.

His letters disgust me.

What has Frank Churchill done to make you suppose him such an *unnatural* creature?

If he had truly wanted to see his father and his new stepmother, he could have contrived it. Not long ago, he was on holiday in Weymouth.

This proves he *can* leave the Churchills.

Yes, sometimes he can.

And those times are whenever he thinks it worth his while, whenever there is any temptation of pleasure.

It isn't fair to judge another's conduct without knowing their situation. We are not acquainted with the steadiness of Mrs. Churchill's temper. He may be able to do more at some times than at others.

There is always one thing a man can do, Emma, and that is *his duty.* Not by maneuvering and finessing, but by *vigor* and *resolution.* It is Frank's duty to attend his father. He knows it to be so, by his promises and messages, but if he really wished to do it, it would be done.

You seem determined to think ill of him.

No, not at all.

I am ready to acknowledge his merits, but I hear of none, other than that he is well-grown and good-looking, with smooth, plausible manners.

If he has *nothing* else to recommend him, he will be a treasure in Highbury. There will be but one subject in all the parishes-- it will be all Frank Churchill and we shall think and speak of nobody else.

You will *excuse* my lack of enthusiasm. If I find him conversable, I shall be happy to know him. But if he is only a chattering coxcomb, he will not long occupy my time or my thoughts.

After several hints from Mr. Knightley that she had been neglecting the Bates ladies--the impoverished widow and her spinster daughter who lived in Highbury--Emma decided to pay a duty call.

It was a disagreeable task; she often found them tiresome, and to her mind they courted every second-rate person in the village.

I am sure Mr. Elton would approve of our visiting the ladies in his stead, would he not?

Mmmm...

I only hope we will be spared a dissection of the latest letter from Jane Fairfax.

Miss Woodhouse! Miss Smith... what a pleasant surprise.

Here, sit by the fire. Shall I place your boots on the fender to dry? Would you care for some sweet cake?

Mrs. Cole has just been here. A pity you missed her. Mr. Cole is busy at his shop, of course, but his wife said he had a letter yesterday from Mr. Elton in Bath.

I believe Mr. Cole is a great friend of Mr. Elton. But then he has so many friends here in the village.

Oh, yes. Our rector is a great favorite wherever he goes.

I recall he even asked me to dance at the Master of Ceremonies Ball. I declined, of course, but such generosity of spirit is quite rare. He is sorely missed.

I vow he has been away an age.

I doubt it has been more than a fortnight...

...bu all hi it mu that a time h

Emma was relieved when the topic of Mr. Elton's absence was exhausted, but was not prepared for Jane Fairfax to succeed him in the conversation.

Speaking of letters, we had one yesterday from my niece. Mrs. Cole was *quite* delighted to hear of it, for Jane is a great favorite of hers. Mrs. Cole shows her nothing but kindness.

I am so happy for you. I hope she is well.

I...I have the letter here somewhere.

I fear I must apologize for Jane's sake for writing such a short letter--only two pages, when in general she fills sheets and sheets and crosses half. Mother often wonders that I can make it out so well.

Miss Fairfax does have beautiful handwriting.

You are so kind. That is high praise coming from you, who write such a fine hand yourself.

Ma'am, did you hear that?

Eh?

Miss Woodhouse has complimented Jane's penmanship!

Mother is a little deaf. Just a trifle. But when Jane comes to visit, she will not find her grandmamma any deafer than she was two years ago

Are you expecting Miss Fairfax here soon?

Yes, next week. We are both delighted...it's been fully two years since her last visit. She is to be with us for three whole months while the Campbells go over to Ireland.

You see, their daughter, *Mrs. Dixon,* has persuaded the Colonel and Mrs. Campbell to visit her there at their country seat in Baly-Craig.

Jane has heard a great deal of its beauty...from *Mr. Dixon.* She often accompanied the Campbell girl while Dixon was courting her, for her parents were *very particular* about her walking out with him alone, and so of course Jane heard everything he told Miss Campbell about his home.

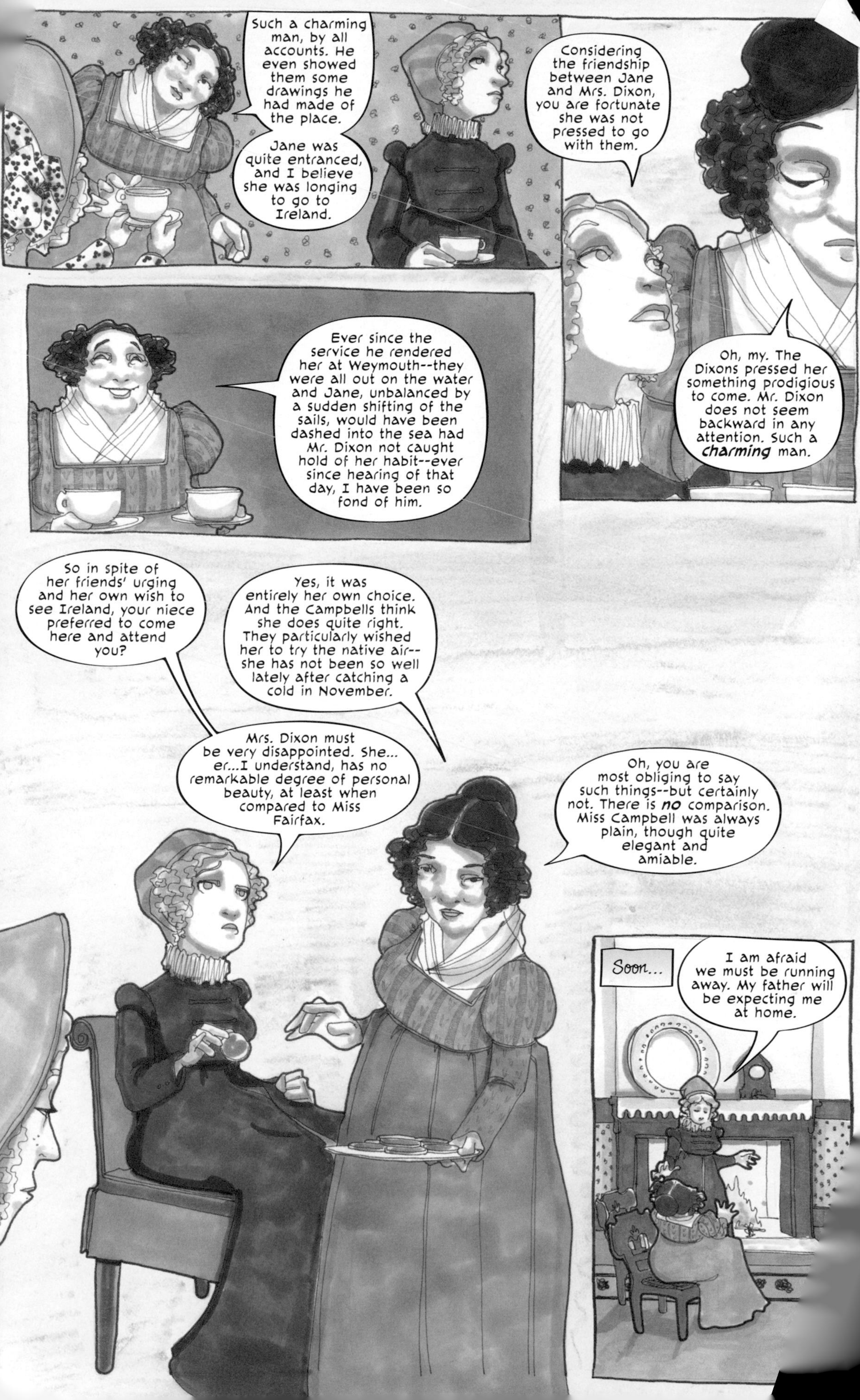
Such a charming man, by all accounts. He even showed them some drawings he had made of the place.
Jane was quite entranced, and I believe she was longing to go to Ireland.
Considering the friendship between Jane and Mrs. Dixon, you are fortunate she was not pressed to go with them.
Oh, my. The Dixons pressed her something prodigious to come. Mr. Dixon does not seem backward in any attention. Such a *charming* man.
Ever since the service he rendered her at Weymouth--they were all out on the water and Jane, unbalanced by a sudden shifting of the sails, would have been dashed into the sea had Mr. Dixon not caught hold of her habit--ever since hearing of that day, I have been so fond of him.
So in spite of her friends' urging and her own wish to see Ireland, your niece preferred to come here and attend you?
Yes, it was entirely her own choice. And the Campbells think she does quite right. They particularly wished her to try the native air--she has not been so well lately after catching a cold in November.
Mrs. Dixon must be very disappointed. She... er...I understand, has no remarkable degree of personal beauty, at least when compared to Miss Fairfax.
Oh, you are most obliging to say such things--but certainly not. There is *no* comparison. Miss Campbell was always plain, though quite elegant and amiable.
Soon...
I am afraid we must be running away. My father will be expecting me at home.

I hope it is not improper of me to ask... but why does Miss Fairfax live with the Campbells and not with her own family?

I do not mind speaking of it. I've heard her history so often from Miss Bates, I know it as though it were my own.

"Jane Fairfax is an orphan, the daughter of an army lieutenant who was killed in battle and of a mother who died grieving her husband. At three, Jane became the ward of her maternal grandmother--Mrs. Bates--here in Highbury. At the time, her prospects were not good."

"But at nine, Jane acquired a benefactor, a Colonel Campbell. He owed a debt to her father, who had nursed the colonel through a camp fever. The Campbells took her under their wing, educated her and treated her like a second daughter."

So she received every advantage.

All but *one.* The little money her father left would not give her independence, and the Colonel could not provide for her--his fortune was bound for his own daughter--so Jane was brought up for educating others.

The Campbells hoped that by giving her the means of becoming a governess or teacher, she would achieve a respectable subsistence.

How she must dread the day she is forced to leave her comfortable home.

So one would think. But I believe she has resolved that within the year she will seek a post as governess...

...even though the Campbells have not pressured her in any way to leave them.

I know you do not care for her, Miss Woodhouse, but I cannot help admiring someone with such... fortitude.

You are entitled to form your own opinions, Harriet. I admit there is little justice to my aversion for Jane Fairfax.

Yet I don't know if I can pay civilities to her for three long months, always doing *more* than I wished and *less* than I ought!

Why **are** my feelings for Jane so fixed? Mr. Knightley believes I dislike her because I see in her the truly accomplished woman I want to be thought myself.

I cannot deny that she is elegant and cultured. In another person, those qualities would gain my highest esteem.

Everyone assumes that because we are of a like age, we must be intimate friends, yet there is such reserve, such coldness in her manner that I feel we are barely acquainted.

A scant week later, Emma found herself sitting opposite Miss Fairfax in the parlor of Hartfield--wondering anew at the young woman's dark beauty--as the other guests made much of her.

At least she is paler than when last I saw her. That is some consolation. Miss Bates said she was ailing and she does, indeed, look unwell.

But, no, I am **determined** to like her. Harriet was right...

When I consider what all this elegance is destined for, what she is going to sink from and how she will be forced to live, I can only feel compassion and respect.

Emma's musings were cut short when the conversation turned to Miss Fairfax's visit to Weymouth. Emma listened attentively, but when Miss Bates told Mr. Knightley of Dixon's rescue of her niece, Jane's cautious reserve returned.

Good man! He clearly has his wits about him.

Indeed, Mr. Dixon did me a very kind service. But it was no more than any gentleman would have done in a similar situation.

Your friend, Mrs. Dixon, is to be felicitated on her recent marriage to such a paragon.

Yes, it was believed by many to be a most suitable match.

I can't help wondering whether Mr. Dixon, perhaps, had been very near changing one friend for the other or been fixed to Miss Campbell only for the sake of the future twelve thousand pounds.

Miss Woodhouse, I'm not sure you heard. My niece had the good fortune to meet Mr. Frank Churchill while she was in Weymouth.

It's true... though I am little acquainted with him.

That's a *deal* more than the rest of us can say. All of Highbury regards you with envy.

I wonder... would you call him handsome?

I believe he was reckoned to be a very fine young man.

And was he agreeable?

He was generally thought so.

And did he appear to be a sensible man, a man of interests and education?

At a watering place it is so hard to decide on such points; manners are all one can safely judge.

I believe everybody found his manners pleasing.

Jane gave not one syllable more of information. Emma, in spite of her resolution to amend past prejudices toward the young woman, felt all her old resentments rise up, all her previous provocations return.

Look at her, wrapped up in a cloak of politeness, determined to hazard nothing. I cannot forgive her.

The morning after Miss Fairfax's visit, Mr. Knightley paid an early call on Mr. Woodhouse and Emma at Hartfield.

Emma, you and Miss Fairfax gave us some very good music last night. I do not know a more luxurious state than being entertained by two such young ladies.

It was kind of you to encourage her to play, since she has no instrument at her grandmother's.

I am happy you approved, Mr. Knightley. I hope I am not deficient in what is due to our guests.

No, you are not often deficient; not often deficient either in manner or comprehension.

Miss Fairfax is... reserved.

You are not going to tell me, that you did not have a pleasant evening.

Oh, no. I was pleased with my own perseverance in asking questions...and amused to think how little information I received.

I am disappointed.

I hope *everybody* had a pleasant evening. Once I rather felt the fire too much, but then moved my chair back. Miss Fairfax must have found the evening agreeable because she had Emma.

True, sir. And Emma, because she had Miss Fairfax.

Emma, I have a bit of news for you. You like news and I heard something this morning that I thought would interest you.

Oh, yes, I do like news. But why do you smile so? Where did you hear it?

But before Mr. Knightley could speak, the breakfast party was interrupted by Miss Bates and her niece, Jane Fairfax.

Oh, my dear sir, how are you this morning? Miss Woodhouse, such a *beautiful* hindquarter of pork you sent us. I am *quite* overpowered!

But have you heard the news...Mr. Elton is to be *married!*

There, that was my news.

But how could you have heard it, sir? I received the news in a note from Mrs. Cole only minutes before we set off for Hartfield. A *Miss Hawkins* from Bath...that's all I know.

I had some business with Cole before I came here. He showed me the letter from Elton.

He will have everybody's wishes for his happiness.

A new neighbor for us all, Miss Woodhouse! Mother is so pleased.

Jane has never met Mr. Elton, but she has a *great* curiosity to see him.

He is the very best young man. And now there will be a *Mrs.* Elton...along with the Coles and the Perrys, who are such happy couples.

I always say, we are blessed in our neighbors.

Is he... ...is he a *tall* man?

Miss Fairfax, you will find after a time here, that Mr. Elton is the standard of perfection, both in *person* and *mind.*

As to *who* or *what* Miss Hawkins is, nothing can be known. It cannot be a very long acquaintance; he has been gone only four weeks.

You are silent, Miss Fairfax. You, who have been so deep in this matrimonial business on Miss Campbell's account, we shall not excuse your being indifferent about Mr. Elton and Miss Hawkins.

When I have met Mr. Elton, I daresay I shall be interested--I believe it requires *that* with me.

As it is some months since Miss Campbell wed, the impression may have worn off a little.

I always fancied Mr. Elton would form an attachment to some young lady hereabouts, that nobody would wonder if he should have aspired to...Ah, Miss Woodhouse lets me chatter on so. She knows I would not offend for the world.

How is Mrs. Knightley and her family? I always pictured Mr. Dixon like Mr. John Knightley...tall and with that sort of look. I'm sure Jane herself remarked on the likeness--

Dear aunt, I never did. I told you Mr. Dixon was plain. Where I have a regard, I always think a person well looking. I gave you what I believed was the *general* opinion when I called him plain.

I see it's coming on to rain, so I'm afraid we must be running away.

Mr. Knightley, if you are leaving also, would you kindly give Jane your arm?

It's a pity young people are in such a *hurry* to marry. And to marry *strangers,* too!

I'm glad Mr. Elton didn't suffer for too long before he found a new interest. But poor Harriet...how downcast she will feel at this news.

After the storm passed, Harriet arrived at her usual time--but in a breathless state.

Oh, Miss Woodhouse... you will *not* believe what has happened. I was taking shelter from the storm at the linen drapers, when Miss Martin and her brother, Mr. Martin, came into the shop. I nearly *fainted!*

She noticed me, but pretended she did not. I am sure he did not see me, for I was standing behind the door.

"But then he *did* notice me, and the two began whispering.

"Presently she approached me and said she was sorry we no longer met. Then Mr. Martin came up to me...

"I vow I could barely *speak* and made some excuse and ran from the store.

"But he followed me outside and said if I was going to Hartfield, I had better go round by Coles Stable, for the closer way was quite flooded with rain.

"He was so considerate... and they were both so pleasant spoken. I would rather *anything* happen to me than have to go through that again."

I'm sure it was distressing, but you behaved extremely well. Console yourself that it is over and can *never*--as a first meeting--occur again. You need not think about it.

But it was all Harriet could speak of, so to distract her, Emma decided to hurry the news of Elton.

Emma was glad that Harriet's encounter with Mr. Martin served to soften the shock of Elton's betrothal, and further assured herself that as Harriet now lived, fully a year might pass without their being thrown together again.

Mr. Elton returned, a very happy man.

Mr. Elton, we were delighted to hear of your engagement to Miss Hawkins. How you must *pine* over being parted from her.

I will be returning to my dear Augusta shortly. I am only here to make arrangements for her comfort at the vicarage.

I am sure Miss Hawkins is both handsome and elegant.

Mr. Cole says that according to the rector, she is also quite accomplished and extremely amiable.

Lucky fellow, that Elton. I understand this Hawkins girl is in possession of an independent fortune.

Oh, yes, *ten thousand a year,* if not more.

As for Emma, she met him briefly in the village...

...and was relieved when the encounter was over.

I wonder that I ever thought him pleasing. He is so inseparably connected with disagreeable feelings, that except as a source of profitable *humiliation,* as a *penance,* I would be thankful if I never saw him again.

At least the presence of a Mrs. Elton will excuse any change of intercourse between us. Former intimacy will sink without remark. And barring her fortune, I doubt Miss Hawkins is Harriet's superior. She is merely the younger daughter of a merchant--it must be called as it is--with no name, no blood, and no alliances.

It's true her sister married well and is rumored to keep two carriages, but that is Augusta Hawkins's only glory.

Miss Martin called on Harriet at Mrs. Goddard's a few days later and, not finding her within, left a note. Harriet quickly became preoccupied over how to respond.

Her visit has to be acknowledged. To neglect mothers and sisters is to show ingratitude. But you must return the visit in such a manner as to convince them that this is a formal acquaintance only.

I believe it will serve if I take you there in the carriage and come back to fetch you a short time later.

Harriet did as she was bid, made a brief appearance at Abbey Mill Farm, and then rejoined Emma in her carriage.

How did it go?

It was... that is, Mrs. Martin and her daughters received me quite coolly... not at all as I was used to.

They spoke only commonplaces... until near the end, when Mrs. Martin remarked that I had grown taller.

"We all went to the wainscot by the window, where *he* had marked my height and his sisters' last summer."

"It...it brought back the memory of that day, a happy day, and suddenly we were all returned to that same good understanding..."

"...but then your carriage drew up and all was over."

This is a bad business. What justifiable resentment they must feel. I would give a great deal to have the Martins rank higher in life, they are so deserving.

But, no. They must be separated, even if there is much pain in the process... so much that I, too, am feeling it.

Emma returned home to a note from the Westons. Frank Churchill was due the very next afternoon!

The following morning she often caught herself looking at the clock and thinking of Mrs. Weston...

But when she went to check on her father in the parlor--

Emma! Allow me to introduce my son, **Frank.** I wrote yesterday he would be here by four o'clock. He actually arrived last night. Imagine the pleasure of coming in upon one's friends before the lookout begins.

It is a great pleasure where one can indulge in it. There are not many houses that I should presume on so far, but in coming **home,** I felt I might do anything.

If Miss Woodhouse would take a turn around the room, perhaps she could answer my many questions about Highbury.

There is so much I want to know... are there pleasant places to walk and ride? Do you ride? Does Highbury afford society and entertainments? Are there musical assemblies and balls?

Yes, on all counts. We go on very well in our little village.

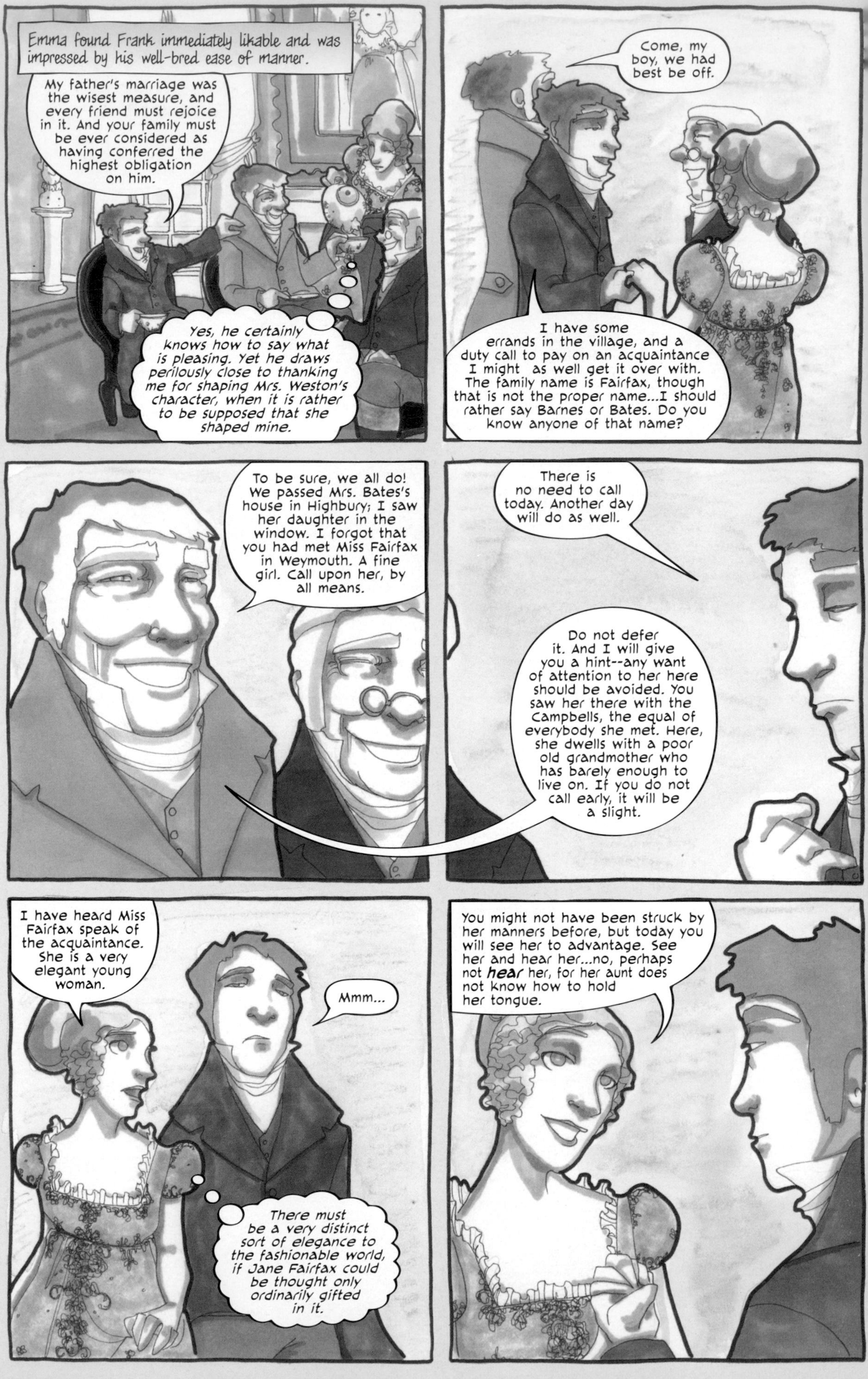
Emma found Frank immediately likable and was impressed by his well-bred ease of manner.
My father's marriage was the wisest measure, and every friend must rejoice in it. And your family must be ever considered as having conferred the highest obligation on him.
Yes, he certainly knows how to say what is pleasing. Yet he draws perilously close to thanking me for shaping Mrs. Weston's character, when it is rather to be supposed that she shaped mine.
Come, my boy, we had best be off.
I have some errands in the village, and a duty call to pay on an acquaintance I might as well get it over with. The family name is Fairfax, though that is not the proper name...I should rather say Barnes or Bates. Do you know anyone of that name?
To be sure, we all do! We passed Mrs. Bates's house in Highbury; I saw her daughter in the window. I forgot that you had met Miss Fairfax in Weymouth. A fine girl. Call upon her, by all means.
There is no need to call today. Another day will do as well.
Do not defer it. And I will give you a hint--any want of attention to her here should be avoided. You saw her there with the Campbells, the equal of everybody she met. Here, she dwells with a poor old grandmother who has barely enough to live on. If you do not call early, it will be a slight.
I have heard Miss Fairfax speak of the acquaintance. She is a very elegant young woman.
Mmm...
There must be a very distinct sort of elegance to the fashionable world, if Jane Fairfax could be thought only ordinarily gifted in it.
You might not have been struck by her manners before, but today you will see her to advantage. See her and hear her...no, perhaps not *hear* her, for her aunt does not know how to hold her tongue.

The following morning, Emma was surprised--and pleased--to see Mrs. Weston and Frank coming up the front drive.

They entreated her to join them on their walk, and Emma was happy to oblige, taking pleasure in showing Frank around the grounds of Hartfield.

I am also curious to see the house where my father lived before he purchased Randalls. And I want to visit the cottage of my old nurse.

These places... these bits of my past...commend themselves to me.

Once they reached Highbury, Frank's interest was drawn to the Crown Inn, a posting house with a large side addition.

It was built many years ago as a ballroom, but its brilliant days have sadly passed away.

I wonder you haven't revived those former days, Miss Woodhouse. I wager there are enough fine houses in the neighborhood to furnish the company required.

I see you have inherited your father's lively spirits. Ah, look, we are but a few doors away from the Bates's home. Did you pay your call yesterday, Mr. Churchill?

I did, indeed. I saw all three ladies, and I am obliged to you for your preparatory hint--else the talking aunt would have taken me by surprise and been the *death* of me!

And how did you think Miss Fairfax looked?

Ill, very ill. That is, if ladies can ever be allowed to look ill. Seriously, she is so naturally pale as to give the appearance of ill health. A most deplorable want of complexion.

Come, admit to me that you admire her except for her complexion.

I cannot separate Miss Fairfax and her complexion.

As they passed Ford's Linen Drapery--a shop his father often spoke of with great fondness-- Frank felt compelled to enter.

Had you known much of Miss Fairfax in Weymouth?

What was that, Miss Woodhouse? You observe me struggling to choose between the cream beaver and the York tan gloves.

Ah, my acquaintance with Jane Fairfax...

That is an unfair question. It is always the lady's right to determine degree of acquaintance. She has undoubtedly told you her account...and I shall not commit myself to claiming more than she would choose to allow.

Upon my word, you answer as discreetly as she does.

Then I will speak the truth. I met her frequently. I knew the Campbells a little in town, and in Weymouth, we were very much in the same set. I liked them all.

You know Miss Fairfax's situation in life, what she is destined to be?

I believe I do.

You tread upon delicate subjects, Emma. Remember that I am here. Mr. Churchill hardly knows what to say when you speak of Miss Fairfax's situation.

I will move a little farther off.

Have you ever heard her play?

Heard her play! I have heard her every year since we began our music lessons. She plays *charmingly.*

I thought so, too. I am fond of music, but have no skill...I--I wanted the opinion of someone who could really judge. A man, a very musical man who was engaged to another, often asked Miss Fairfax to play, even to the point of preferring her to his betrothed. That, I thought, was some proof.

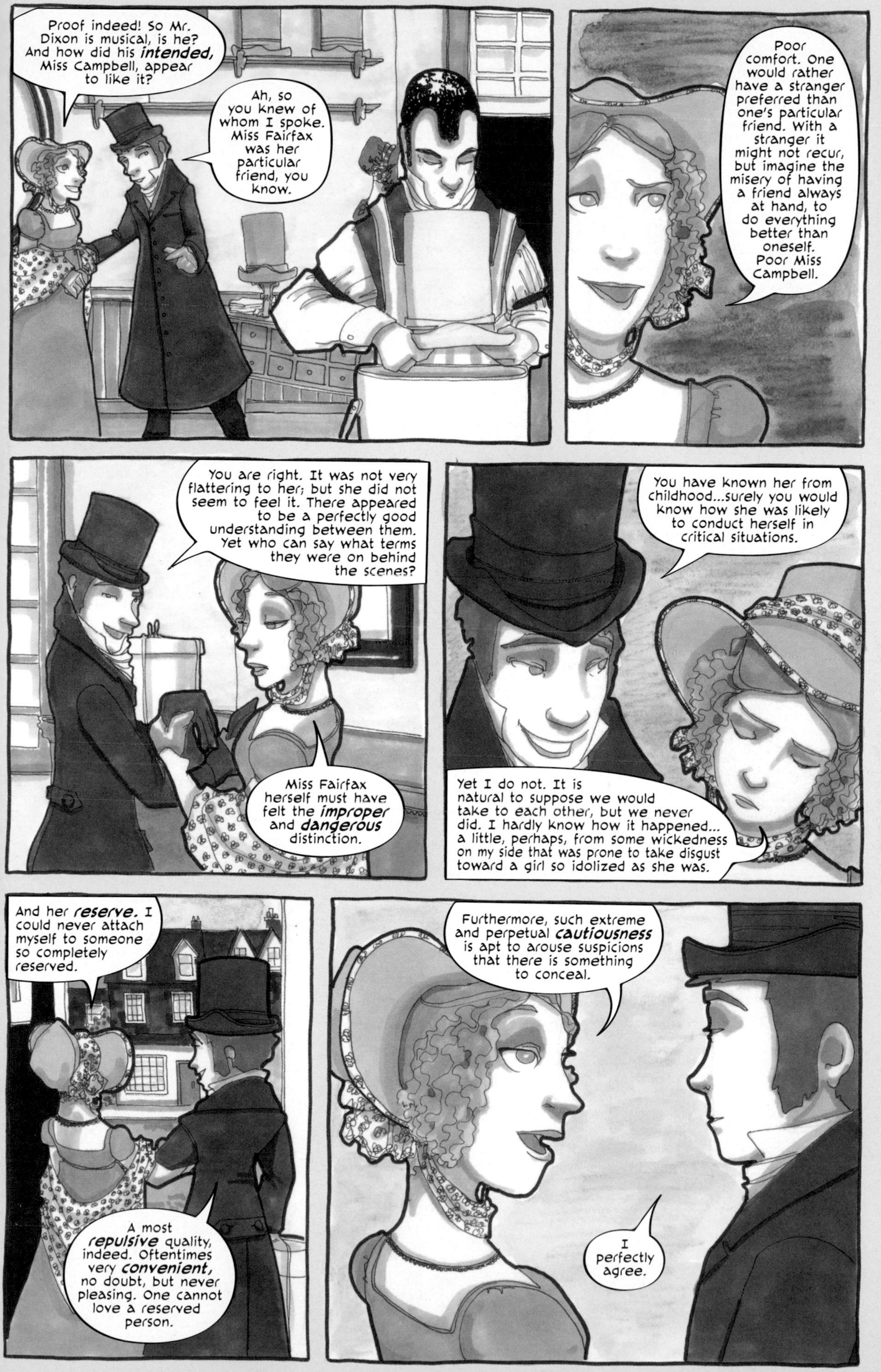
Proof indeed! So Mr. Dixon is musical, is he? And how did his *intended,* Miss Campbell, appear to like it?
Ah, so you knew of whom I spoke. Miss Fairfax was her particular friend, you know.
Poor comfort. One would rather have a stranger preferred than one's particular friend. With a stranger it might not recur, but imagine the misery of having a friend always at hand, to do everything better than oneself. Poor Miss Campbell.
You are right. It was not very flattering to her; but she did not seem to feel it. There appeared to be a perfectly good understanding between them. Yet who can say what terms they were on behind the scenes?
Miss Fairfax herself must have felt the *improper* and *dangerous* distinction.
You have known her from childhood...surely you would know how she was likely to conduct herself in critical situations.
Yet I do not. It is natural to suppose we would take to each other, but we never did. I hardly know how it happened... a little, perhaps, from some wickedness on my side that was prone to take disgust toward a girl so idolized as she was.
And her *reserve.* I could never attach myself to someone so completely reserved.
A most *repulsive* quality, indeed. Oftentimes very *convenient,* no doubt, but never pleasing. One cannot love a reserved person.
Furthermore, such extreme and perpetual *cautiousness* is apt to arouse suspicions that there is something to conceal.
I perfectly agree.

Emma's good opinion of Frank Churchill was shaken the next day, when she learned he had gone to London for a haircut. There was an air of foppery and nonsense in it that she could not approve.

The boy's clearly a coxcomb.

All young people will have their little whims.

Hum! Just the trifling silly fellow I took him for.

In other news, are you attending the Coles dinner party, Emma?

Mr. Weston and I have been invited and are looking forward to it.

My invitation arrived at Donwell three days past.

I knew of this party weeks ago, but determined I should not go. For all that the Coles are respectable, someone ought to teach them it is not fitting to presume upon the superior families of Highbury.

Still, I wonder why *we* have not received an invitation.

Dear me...it completely slipped my mind. Emma, an invitation came in this morning's post.

Ah, but I am not fond of dinner visiting. Never was. Yet I cannot wish to prevent Emma from going.

But, Papa--I have no wish to--

I would be happy to take your place as Emma's chaperon, sir, and furthermore, I will ask Mrs. Goddard to sit with you on the night of the party.

Then Emma may go with my blessing...provided she comes away the instant she grows tired.

And so Emma found her resistance overruled by the good intentions of others.

Frank Churchill himself called the very next day.

You behold me, shorn and undaunted by all the tittle-tattle. Did my barber live *twice* the distance from Highbury, I would still seek out his good services.

Silly things cease to be silly if done by sensible people in an impudent way. Wickedness is always wickedness, but folly is not always folly.

The day of the Coles' party arrived.

Ah, Mr. Knightley arrives in style for a change. In my opinion, he is too apt to get about as he can--insisting on walking everywhere until his boots are in a state--and not using his carriage so often as becomes the owner of Donwell Abbey.

This is coming as you should do, like a gentleman. I am quite glad to see you.

How lucky that we should arrive at the same time. If we had met first in the drawing room, I doubt you would have discerned me to be more of a gentleman than usual.

There is *always* a look of self-consciousness when people come in a way they know is beneath them. I daresay you carry it off, with a sort of bravado. But now you have nothing to try for. Now I shall be happy to walk into the same room with you.

Nonsensical girl!

Mr. Churchill was seated beside Emma at dinner, a pairing, she suspected, that owed itself to some manipulation on his part.

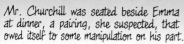

I understand they had to restrict the dinner guests and so invited Miss Bates, Miss Fairfax and Miss Smith for later this evening.

I admit I am glad. It allows me your undivided attention.

The table conversation remained general, ranging from politics to Mr. Elton--but Emma's interest was roused when Mrs. Cole mentioned Jane Fairfax.

I was calling on Miss Bates and Miss Fairfax yesterday, when I was struck by the sight of a fine pianoforte in their parlor. It had apparently arrived the day before...to the astonishment of both aunt and niece.

They at last decided it could only be from one quarter, Colonel Campbell. Yet it seems Jane had a letter from him just the day before and no mention was made of the instrument. Perhaps he chose to surprise her.

Why do you smile?

Nay, why do you?

Me? I suppose I smile in pleasure at Colonel Campbell's being so rich and liberal.

Though I wonder they never offered her one *before* now.

Perhaps Miss Fairfax has never been staying here so long. And yet you continue to look suspicious, and I venture that whatever you suspect, I too shall suspect.

Perhaps it was a gift from Mrs. Dixon. The mode and mystery of it is more like a woman's scheme.

If so, you must extend your suspicions to *Mr. Dixon*. We were speaking the other day of his being a warm admirer of her playing.

Yes, and what you told me confirmed an idea I had entertained before. What if, after courting her friend, Mr. Dixon had the misfortune to fall in *love* with Miss Fairfax? Or that he became conscious of an attachment on her side.

I am sure there must be a reason for her choosing to come to Highbury instead of going to Ireland with the Campbells. As to the pretense of her coming here for the native air-- in the summer it might have passed, but what can native air do in January?

I...I do not require you to adopt my suspicions--

Upon my word, they have an air of great probability. Mr. Dixon's preference for her music was very decided.

The arrival of this piano is *decisive* with me. I wanted to know a little more, and this tells me *quite* enough.

A short time after the ladies from Highbury arrived, Mrs. Weston sought out Emma.

My dear Emma, I have been making discoveries and I must tell them while my thoughts are fresh. Do you know how Miss Bates and her niece came here?

They walked, I conclude. How else could they come?

So I thought myself. But when I offered Miss Fairfax the use of our carriage to convey her home--for she appears almost feverish tonight--she thanked me and said that *Mr. Knightley's* carriage had brought them and was to take them home again.

That is just the sort of thing Mr. Knightley would do. He is not a gallant man, but he is very humane.

You give him credit for more simple disinterested benevolence than I do. An idea darted into my head, and I have not been able to get it out again. In short, I have made a match between *Mr. Knightley* and *Jane Fairfax.*

See the consequence of keeping you company! What do you say to it?

Dear Mrs. Weston, how could you *think* of such a thing? Mr. Knightley must not marry! Would you have little Henry cut out from inheriting Donwell Abbey? No, I cannot at all consent to Mr. Knightley's marrying.

I do not *want* the match...but if Mr. Knightley wished to marry, you would not have him refrain on account of a child who knows nothing of the matter.

Yes, I would. I have never had such an idea and cannot adopt it now. And Jane, too, of all women.

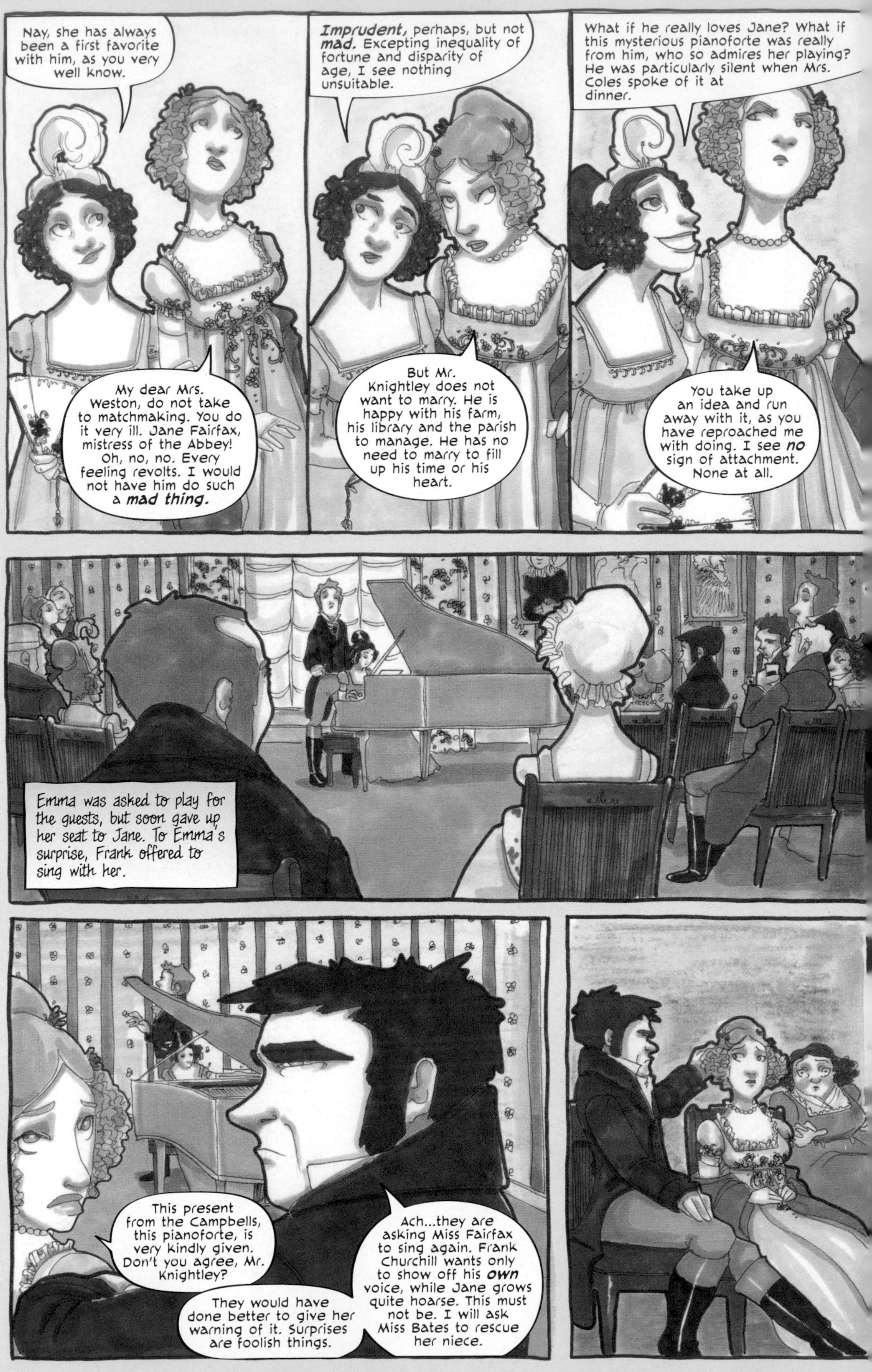

Nay, she has always been a first favorite with him, as you very well know.
My dear Mrs. Weston, do not take to matchmaking. You do it very ill. Jane Fairfax, mistress of the Abbey! Oh, no, no. Every feeling revolts. I would not have him do such a *mad thing.*
Imprudent, perhaps, but not *mad.* Excepting inequality of fortune and disparity of age, I see nothing unsuitable.
But Mr. Knightley does not want to marry. He is happy with his farm, his library and the parish to manage. He has no need to marry to fill up his time or his heart.
What if he really loves Jane? What if this mysterious pianoforte was really from him, who so admires her playing? He was particularly silent when Mrs. Coles spoke of it at dinner.
You take up an idea and run away with it, as you have reproached me with doing. I see *no* sign of attachment. None at all.
Emma was asked to play for the guests, but soon gave up her seat to Jane. To Emma's surprise, Frank offered to sing with her.
This present from the Campbells, this pianoforte, is very kindly given. Don't you agree, Mr. Knightley?
They would have done better to give her warning of it. Surprises are foolish things.
Ach...they are asking Miss Fairfax to sing again. Frank Churchill wants only to show off his *own* voice, while Jane grows quite hoarse. This must not be. I will ask Miss Bates to rescue her niece.

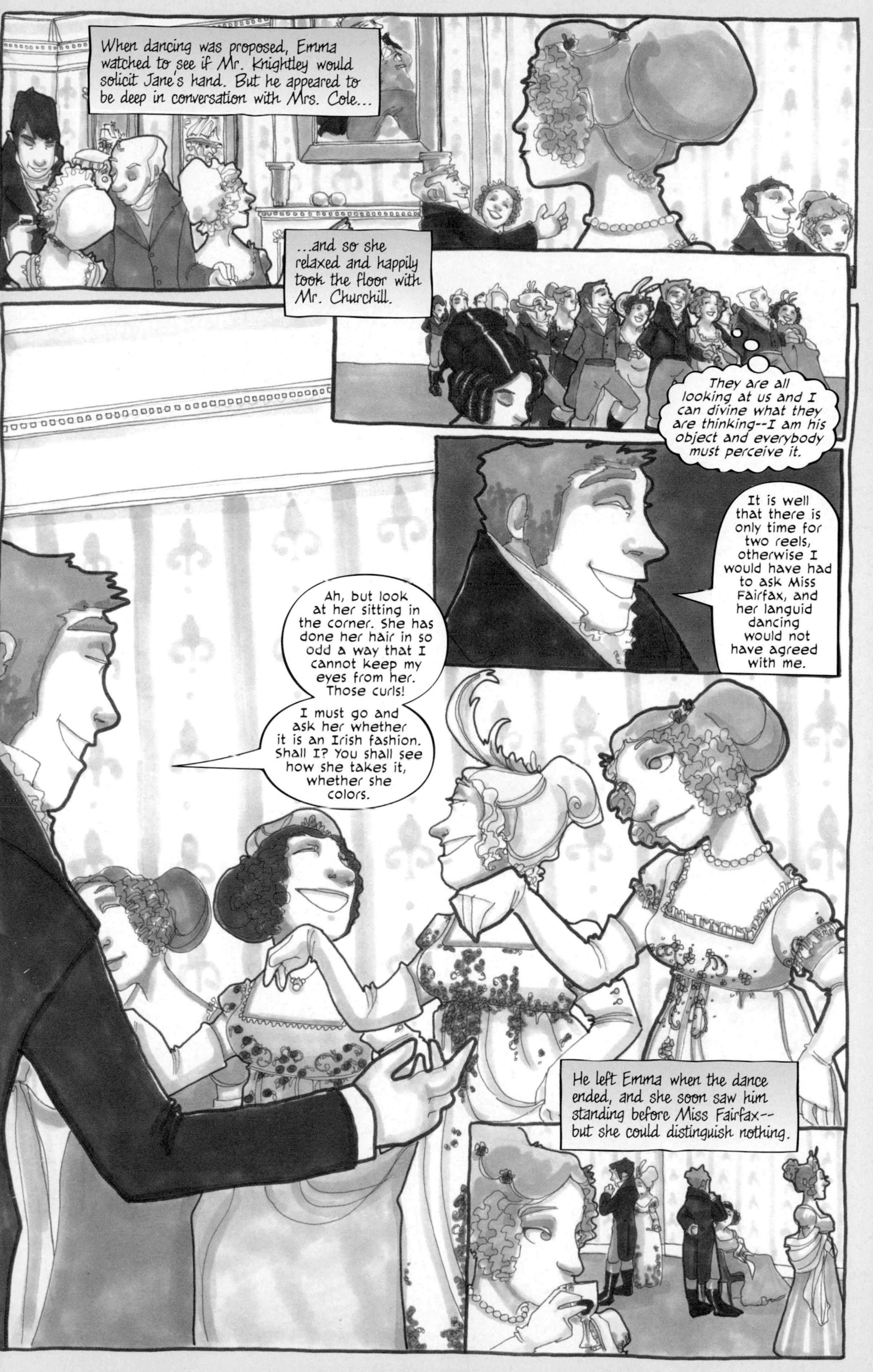
When dancing was proposed, Emma watched to see if Mr. Knightley would solicit Jane's hand. But he appeared to be deep in conversation with Mrs. Cole...
...and so she relaxed and happily took the floor with Mr. Churchill.
They are all looking at us and I can divine what they are thinking--I am his object and everybody must perceive it.
It is well that there is only time for two reels, otherwise I would have had to ask Miss Fairfax, and her languid dancing would not have agreed with me.
Ah, but look at her sitting in the corner. She has done her hair in so odd a way that I cannot keep my eyes from her. Those curls!
I must go and ask her whether it is an Irish fashion. Shall I? You shall see how she takes it, whether she colors.
He left Emma when the dance ended, and she soon saw him standing before Miss Fairfax--but she could distinguish nothing.

The next morning, Harriet asked Emma to accompany her to Ford's, and Emma agreed, thinking she could protect her friend if Mr. Martin should appear.

I saw Miss Cox yesterday...she told me Mr. Martin had been to dine with her family on Sunday and sat next to her.

I believe she or her sister would be very glad to marry him.

Quite likely. I am sure they are the most *vulgar* girls in Highbury.

When Harriet took too long with her purchases...

...Emma decided to wait outside and watch the passing scene.

We are on our way to Hartfield, but decided to visit the Bates ladies first and hear the new pianoforte.

I would be happy to wait here with Miss Woodhouse, ma'am, and meet you later at Hartfield.

I thought you meant to go with me, Frank. They would be very pleased to see you.

Me? I should be quite in the way. I shall be no support to you, Mrs. Weston. I am the most *wretched* being in the world at a civil falsehood.

I am persuaded you can be as insincere as your neighbors, when it is necessary.

Very well, ma'am, I will go, but only because I have the hope of Hartfield as a reward.

As Harriet was settling her account, Miss Bates appeared in the shop.

Miss Woodhouse, I have just run across the street to entreat you to come sit with us a little while and give your opinion of the new instrument. Mr. Churchill said your appraisal was worth having...

I asked him to come with me to persuade you, but he said he was busy fixing the rivet on Mother's spectacles.

Can you imagine him sitting there, so intent on helping us? So very *obliging*... and when I brought out the baked apples, he said they were the finest he ever tasted.

Jane served them to Mr. Knightley when he called last week and told him how much she enjoys them. He remarked that we must be near the end of our stock.

I admitted that, sadly, we were...and he offered to send us a fresh supply.

Jane nearly quarreled with me over that, preferring that I made him believe we had a great many left.

They entered the parlor and found Frank Churchill still working on the spectacles.

Have you not finished yet? You would not make a very good living as a silversmith.

I have not been working uninterrupted. I had to help Miss Fairfax, who was trying to make her instrument stand steadily. There is an unevenness in the floor.

I believe you fixed it, Mr. Churchill.

Your benefactor chose well. I heard a good deal of Colonel Campbell's taste in Weymouth and I'm sure this pianoforte is exactly what he--and all his party--would prize.

It is not fair to tease her. Mine was a random guess. Do not distress her.

How much your friends in Ireland must be enjoying your pleasure. Do you imagine Colonel Campbell knows the business going forward at this time?

Until I have a letter from him, I can imagine nothing. It must all be conjecture.

Aye, sometimes one conjectures right, and sometimes one conjectures wrong...What *nonsense* one talks, Miss Woodhouse, when one is hard at work.

There, it is done. I have the pleasure, Mrs. Bates, of restoring your spectacles, healed for the present.

Play something now...if you are very kind it will be one of the tunes we danced to... last night. Let me live them over again. You did not enjoy them as I did; you appeared tired.

I believe you were glad we danced no longer, but I would have given worlds-- all the worlds one has to give--for one half hour more.

What felicity to hear a tune again that has made one happy. If I'm not mistaken, that was danced at Weymouth.

When Miss Fairfax began to play again, Mr. Churchill returned to Emma's side.

You speak too plain. She must understand you. I...I am ashamed and wish I had never taken up the idea.

She is not entirely without fault. She is playing Robert Adair now, *his* favorite.

Suddenly Miss Bates gave a crow of delight--

Oh, look, it's Mr. Knightley! Yoo-hoo! Oh, do come up.

I'm off to Kingston... but perhaps for five minutes, in case you have errands for me.

Miss Woodhouse is here...and Mr. Churchill.

Oh. Sorry, no. I must go. Another time.

Did you hear his kind offer to run errands for us in Kingston?

We heard his offer. We heard everything.

Frank Churchill had danced once at Highbury and longed to dance again. He broached this desire to Emma one night at Randalls.

It would be delightful if the same company from the Coles's party could be gathered here for a dance.

That is a capital idea! I would be happy to play as long as you wished to dance.

But will there be good room here for nine or ten couples? Perhaps we could open the doors between two parlors.

There will be severe drafts then, and I could not bear it for Emma. She is bound to catch cold...you know she is not strong.

After much discussion, it was decided the best option was to hold the ball at the Crown Inn, with Mrs. Weston directing the whole.

I shall write at once to Enscombe, asking to extend my stay. They will not refuse me such a *delightful* opportunity.

Once Frank's request had been answered--his aunt was not pleased, but she did not oppose him--he and Emma began to plan.

Mrs. Weston suggested serving only sandwiches and punch.

Never say so! A ball without supper is an infamous *fraud* on the rights of men and women.

Mr. Knightley, provokingly, did not enter into the spirit of the event.

A ball at the Crown? You know I rarely dance.

Still, if the Westons think a ball worth all this trouble, I have nothing to say against it. But I would rather spend the evening at home with my accounts.

I happen to know that Miss Fairfax is looking forward to it with great pleasure.

I cannot refuse to attend... and I will endeavor to keep awake as much as possible.

Three days of delightful anticipation on Emma's part were immediately followed by the overthrow of everything.

I fear I must depart for Enscombe within the hour. My uncle writes that my aunt is ailing -though her illnesses generally occur for her own *convenience.* Oh, of all horrid things, leave-taking is the *worst.*

But you will come again. This will not be your only visit. Oh, but our poor ball must be quite given up.

Ah! That ball! *Why* did we wait and not hold it at once? If I can come again, we are still to have it.

And must you be off this morning? No time to spare for Miss Bates or Miss Fairfax? You wouldn't want to slight them.

I stopped in there already. I was passing their door and thought it better to pay my visit then--

Uh...in short... Miss Woodhouse, I think you can hardly be quite without suspicion--

=Ahem=

He is more in love with me than I had supposed.

It was something to feel that all the rest of my time might be given to Hartfield. My...my *regard* for Hartfield is most warm--ah, but here is my father to fetch me.

Goodbye, then. I shall hear about you all from Mrs. Weston. That is my chief consolation.

I must be a *little* in love with him...

No, sadly, we've heard nothing yet.

Have you heard from Mr. Churchill, is he in good spirits? What are the chances of his coming to Randalls this spring?

Emma continued to entertain no doubt of her being in love with Mr. Churchill and eagerly sought news of him from Mrs. Weston.

On the other hand, she could not admit herself unhappy or less disposed for employment than usual.

I *do* miss him, but it's odd that I don't ever find myself using the word *sacrifice*. I suspect he is not really necessary to my happiness. I certainly will not persuade myself to feel more than I do. I am quite enough in love and should be sorry to be more.

In truth, after every fancied or imagined declaration on his part, I *refuse* him. Surely a strong attachment would produce more of a struggle than any I foresee.

He is undoubtedly very much in love--everything indicates it.

When he comes again, I must be on my guard not to encourage it now that I have made up my mind. Any affection he feels must subside into friendship.

As for myself, I shall do very well again after a little while, and then it will be a good thing over. They say everyone is in love once in their lives, and I shall have been let off easily.

When a letter from Frank did arrive, Mrs. Weston happily shared it with Emma.

See here, he laments that he had no time to bid farewell to your "beautiful little friend" Miss Smith. He asks you to make his apologies to her.

Is it possible Harriet might *succeed* me in his affections? Oh, I know the danger of indulging in such speculation, but *stranger* things have happened.

When Mr. Elton returned to Highbury with his new bride, Emma and Harriet decided to get the awkward business over with and call on them.

As we passed Hartfield on our way into the village, Miss Woodhouse, I remarked to Mr. E. that it was very like Maple Grove, the home of my sister's husband. "Very like, indeed," he assured me. Though I believe the grounds of Maple Grove are more *extensive*, Hartfield certainly has a *tidy* and *charming* aspect.

Speaking of my sister and Mr. Suckling, they have promised to visit us this spring. I will *recommend* they bring the barouche-landau rather than their chaise so that we may explore the neighborhood. We explored King's Weston twice last summer.

You do have coaching parties here, do you not, Miss Woodhouse?

No, not as a rule. We are some distance from the striking beauties that most coaching parties seek out. We are a very quiet set of people, I believe, who enjoy our *home* comforts.

Never believe it. There are *plenty* of scenic vistas hereabouts and plenty of people likewise inclined to view them.

Nobody can be more devoted to home than *I* am. I was quite the *proverb* for it at Maple Grove. My sister was often heard to remark that she could barely budge me past the railings.

Alas, one also needs to mix in the world to a proper degree. What a *hardship* it must be, Miss Woodhouse, to have your activities so *curtailed* by your father's indifferent health.

Indifferent? I would hardly say so.

You should take him to Bath, my dear. The waters are quite *miraculous*... and I would be happy to put you in touch with my friend, Mrs. Partridge, who owns a lodging house there.

Emma forcibly restrained herself from saying something impolite—so incensed was she at the notion of being escorted anywhere by a landlady.

We called on the Westons yesterday-- such a *pleasant* couple.

Mrs. Weston was your governess, I think? I certainly was astonished to find her so...um... *ladylike.*

Mrs. Weston's manners--her *propriety, simplicity* and *elegance*-- have always been particularly good.

And you will never guess who came in while we were there. *Knightley* himself! Mr. E. has often spoken of him, of course, and I can say now that my *caro sposo* need not be ashamed of his friend. Knightley is quite the gentleman.

Happily for Emma, it was now time to be off.

Insufferable woman. Worse than I expected. *Knightley!* Never seen him before in her life, yet calls him "Knightley." A *vulgar* little upstart, with all her *Mr. E.* and *caro sposo*...to proclaim Knightley a gentleman. I doubt he returned the compliment and labeled her a *lady.*

I thought she was at least pretty.

And Mrs. Weston... astonished that the person who brought me up should be a gentlewoman! Worse and worse. I never met her equal, Harriet.

Emma discovered, during their subsequent encounters, that she was not required to retract her ill opinion. Mrs. Elton remained self-important, presuming, ignorant, and ill-bred. Worse yet, both husband and wife treated Harriet with open disdain.

Oh, Miss Smith...I vow I didn't see you there.

Some people simply refuse to wait their turn.

When the woman's many proposals of intimacy to Emma fell upon stony ground, Mrs. Elton turned her attention to Jane Fairfax.

Miss Fairfax is absolutely *charming!* So mild and ladylike, such talent and accomplishments. And her situation is so *affecting.* We must endeavor to do something for her, bring her forward.

When you understand what her home life has been with the Campbells, you will see that her talents can hardly be unknown.

Ah, but she is in such *obscurity* now, so thrown away. Her advantages are at an end. I am sure she feels it... she is so *timid.*

I am not aware of how you, or those who have known her longer than you, can show her any other attention than--

A vast deal may be done by those who dare to act. You and I shall set an example and many will follow as far as they can, though they do not have our advantages.

I shall invite her to dine, have musical parties to display her talents, and introduce her wherever I can. My acquaintance is so extensive, I am sure I shall hear of something to suit her before long.

Poor Jane! You did nothing to *deserve* this. You might have done wrong to Mrs. Dixon, but this is a punishment beyond what you have merited. The kindness and protection of Mrs. Elton!

Before long, Highbury grew used to the sight of Miss Fairfax at the side of the rector's wife.

Miss Bates says the Campbells are prolonging their visit to Ireland and have implored Jane to join them. Yet she prefers to stay here under privations of every sort.

She must have a powerful motive for refusing their invitation, for choosing to remain here and endure the *penury* of Mrs. Elton's conversation--

Perhaps visiting the vicarage is better than always being at home. Her aunt is a good creature, but can be a *tiresome* companion. We must consider what Miss Fairfax quits before we *condemn* her for where she goes.

You are correct, Mrs. Weston. Jane Fairfax is as capable as any of us of forming an opinion of Mrs. Elton. Could she have chosen with whom to associate, she would not have chosen her...

But she receives attentions from Mrs. Elton that nobody else pays her.

Mr. Knightley, such attentions, I imagine, would *disgust* rather than *gratify* Miss Fairfax.

You may be sure that Mrs. Elton treats her with respect, Emma--it is clear she awes Mrs. Elton with her superiority of mind and manner.

I know how *highly* you think of Miss Fairfax. And yet one day the extent of your admiration may take you by *surprise.*

So you have been settling that I should marry Miss Fairfax?

Indeed not. You have scolded me too much for matchmaking to take such a liberty. One...says these meaningless things. I don't wish you to marry Jane Fairfax or Jane *anybody.*

No, I doubt my admiration will take me by surprise. She is a charming young woman, but not without *fault.* She has not the open temper one could wish for in a wife.

In spite of her dislike of Mrs. Elton, Emma felt duty bound to hold a dinner party in the Eltons' honor.

Ah, Miss Woodhouse...such a *fine* house. I could almost fancy myself at Maple Grove. As soon as I entered, I observed how very like the staircase is, placed exactly in the same part of the hall.

Miss Fairfax, your aunt told me you went to fetch your mail this morning in the rain. This must not be! Young ladies should take care of themselves; they are delicate plants.

I always fetch the letters when I am here, Mr. Woodhouse. A walk before breakfast does me good.

The post office holds some charm at one period in our lives. But when you are *my* age, you won't think letters are worth going through the rain for.

Going in the rain for letters? Miss Fairfax, this must not be. It is a sign I was not there to take care of you. I shall speak to Mr. E. He will see that the man--or one of our men, I forget his name--who fetches our mail shall bring yours as well.

You are very kind, but I would not give up my morning walk. I am advised to be out of doors as much as I can, and the post office is as fine an object as any.

Nonsense. The thing is quite determined--as far as I can determine anything without the approval of my lord and master.

Excuse me, I cannot consent to such an arrangement, to needlessly trouble your servant.

On the contrary, it is a *kindness* to employ our men.

The post office is a **wonderful** thing. So seldom do letters go astray. When one considers the hands--and bad hands--the clerks must decipher, it increases the wonder.

I have heard it asserted that the same sort of handwriting often prevails in families. Though that must apply to **females**. Males get very little schooling in the subject and scramble into any hand they find.

Isabella and Emma, I think, do write very much alike. I have not always known their writing apart.

Yes, there is a likeness. Though Emma's hand is the stronger.

I never saw any gentleman's hand to equal...that is...er...Mr. Frank Churchill writes one of the best gentleman's hands I ever **saw**.

I do not admire it. It wants strength. It is like a **woman's** writing.

It by no means wants strength. It is not a large hand, but very clear and certainly strong.

Mrs. Weston, do you not have a letter of his with you?

No, alas. I answered his last letter and put it away.

I have a note from him in my desk. I shall show it to Mr. Knightley after dinner and convince him.

Oh! When a **gallant** like Mr. Churchill writes to a **fair lady** like Miss Woodhouse, he will of course put forth his **best**.

After dinner...

Ah, here it is come April, and I gather you have heard nothing back from your inquiries for a governess position, Jane.

I have not made any inquiries. I do not wish to make any yet, not until the Campbells return.

My dear, you cannot begin too soon. You are not aware of the *difficulty* in procuring exactly the desirable position.

I, not aware! Who can have thought of it as I have?

I shall write to Mrs. Partridge in Bath, charging her to be on the lookout for anything eligible.

Thank you, but I would rather you didn't mention it to her at present.

You don't know how many candidates there are for the *first* situations...My brother's cousin Mrs. Bragge had an *infinity* of applicants, for she moves in the first circles. That is the sort of situation I desire for you.

Your inexperience really amuses me. A situation such as you deserve is not an everyday occurrence. We must begin *at once.*

When the time is right, there are places in town where inquiries will soon produce something. Offices for the sale of-- not quite of human *flesh*--but of human *intellect.*

Human flesh! My dear, you shock me. Do you mean a fling at the *slave* trade?

I meant only the *governess* trade. Widely different as to the guilt of those who carry it on. But as to the misery of its victims, who can say?

As the gentlemen entered the drawing room, Mr. Weston came forward to speak to Emma and his wife.

What do you think? You've just had a note delivered from *Frank.* I took the liberty of opening it...he is coming, do you see? I always knew he would be here again soon.

He writes that the Churchills will be staying in London for a time--in consideration of Mrs. Churchill's health. How *wonderful* for you both. He will be able to ride here as often as he likes.

Or as often as *she* allows him.

I shall look forward to meeting young Mr. Churchill at Randalls. Mr. E. and I will lose no time in calling upon him.

He should be in London early next week. They are coming down from Enscombe, in Yorkshire.

Ah, sixty miles farther from London than Maple Grove. But what is distance to people of large fortune? You would be amazed how my brother, Mr. Suckling, flies about.

The evil of the distance is that Mrs. Churchill is unwell and can barely leave her couch. Yet to London she will come.

Perhaps she is weary of her home. Even a fine home can be very retired. Nothing can stand more retired from the road than Maple Grove.

Such an *immense* plantation all around it! Not every woman has the health or spirits of my sister to enjoy such *seclusion.*

When your son does come again, he will find an addition to Highbury--if I may call myself an *addition.* Then again, he may have never heard of there being such a creature.

Dear madam! Mrs. Weston's letters lately have been full of little else *but* Mrs. Elton.

I hope you will be pleased with my son. He is thought to be a fine young man, but he is no *prodigy.*

I have heard *much* in praise of him. But I ought to warn you, I always judge for myself. I am no flatterer.

In his favor, he is devoted to Mrs. Churchill, who has cared for him all these years. Sadly, she is not in my good graces.

She was a *nobody* when my late wife's brother married her, but ever since being turned into a Churchill, she has out-Churchill'd them all in high and mighty claims. But in *herself,* I assure you, she is an upstart.

How *provoking* that must be! I have quite a *horror* of upstarts. There was an odious, encroaching family that lived near Maple Grove--

Oh, look, here's the tea tray.

Once the guests were gone, Emma grappled with her agitation at hearing the news of Mr. Churchill.

I shall be very glad to see him...Oh, but I *do* hope he does not return with the same warmth of sentiment that he took *away.* If two months of separation have not cooled him, there are *dangers* before me.

I do not intend for my affections to get *entangled* again, nor do I want to encourage his. At all costs, I must try to keep him from an absolute declaration.

Yet I cannot help feeling the spring will not pass without a crisis, some event to alter my *tranquility.*

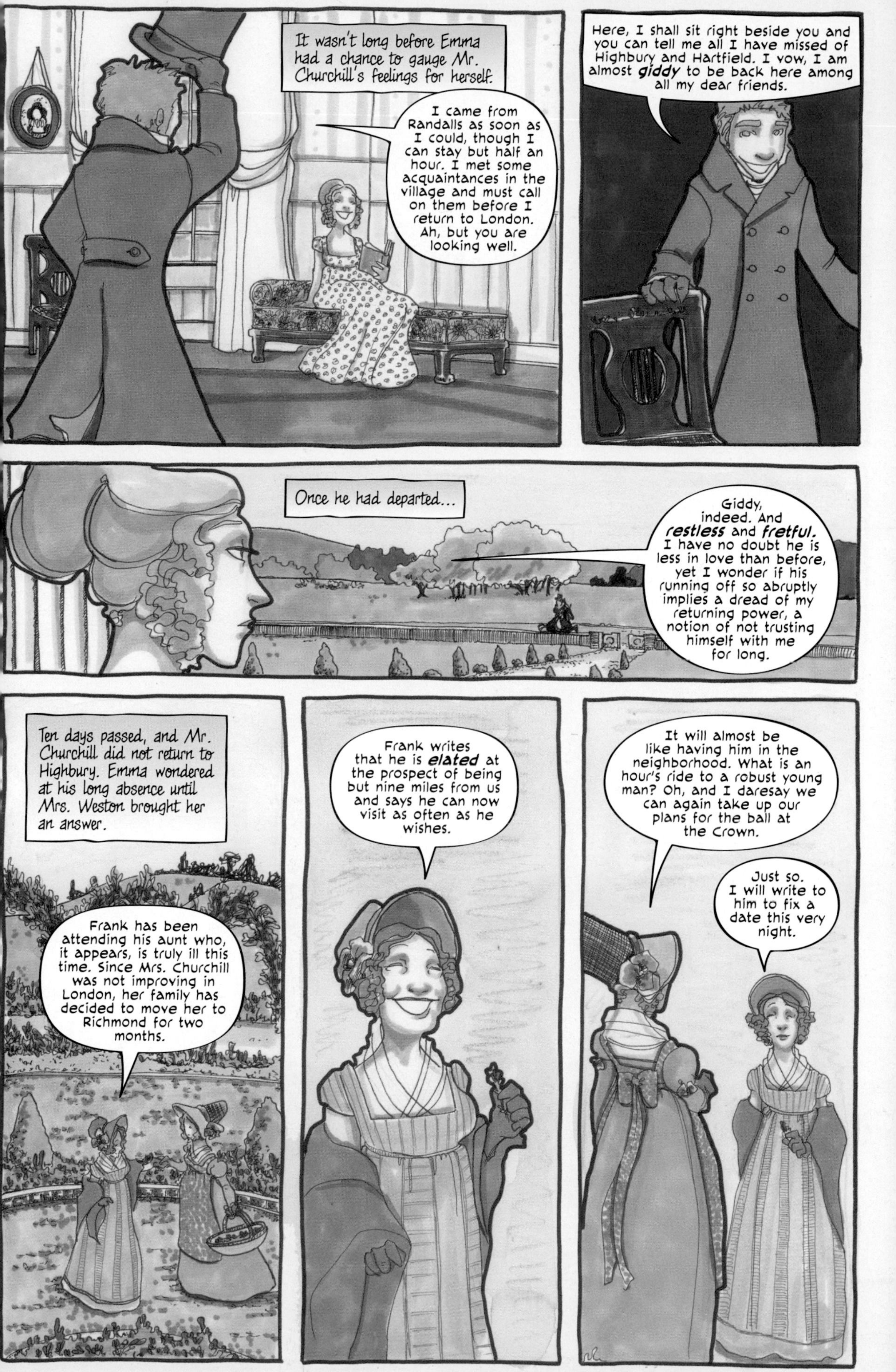

It wasn't long before Emma had a chance to gauge Mr. Churchill's feelings for herself.
I came from Randalls as soon as I could, though I can stay but half an hour. I met some acquaintances in the village and must call on them before I return to London. Ah, but you are looking well.
Here, I shall sit right beside you and you can tell me all I have missed of Highbury and Hartfield. I vow, I am almost giddy to be back here among all my dear friends.
Once he had departed...
Giddy, indeed. And restless and fretful. I have no doubt he is less in love than before, yet I wonder if his running off so abruptly implies a dread of my returning power, a notion of not trusting himself with me for long.
Ten days passed, and Mr. Churchill did not return to Highbury. Emma wondered at his long absence until Mrs. Weston brought her an answer.
Frank has been attending his aunt who, it appears, is truly ill this time. Since Mrs. Churchill was not improving in London, her family has decided to move her to Richmond for two months.
Frank writes that he is elated at the prospect of being but nine miles from us and says he can now visit as often as he wishes.
It will almost be like having him in the neighborhood. What is an hour's ride to a robust young man? Oh, and I daresay we can again take up our plans for the ball at the Crown.
Just so. I will write to him to fix a date this very night.

No misfortune occurred to prevent the ball at the Crown. Emma arrived early--at the Westons' request--to offer an opinion on the propriety and comfort of the room.

So, what do you think of their arrangements? Though I warn you, with or without your approval, I intend to have a delightful evening.

All is just as it should be.

As the guests began to arrive, Mr. Churchill grew restless, always watching the doorway.

You seem distracted. Are you expecting someone?

I have a great *curiosity* to see Mrs. Elton. It cannot be long before she comes.

Here they are now...Ah! but what is wrong?

The Eltons are *alone!* They were to have brought Miss Bates and Miss Fairfax in their carriage.

It is of no mind. I will ask them to send the carriage back. Meanwhile, *you* entertain the Eltons... I am longing to know what you think of them.

Mrs. Elton soon revealed her opinion of Frank Churchill...

A very fine young man. You may believe me, for I *never* offer idle compliments. So truly the gentleman, without conceit or puppyism. I have a vast dislike of puppies...as does my brother, Mr. Suckling--

Oh, look! Miss Bates and Miss Fairfax have arrived. What a *pleasure* it is to send one's carriage for a friend! I understand you also offered, Mr. Weston, but you may be sure I will *always* take care of them.

Later that evening...

Nobody can think less of dress in general than *I* do, but upon this occasion, which I have no doubt was arranged to honor me, I would not wish to be *inferior* to others. And I see very few pearls in the room...

So Frank Churchill is a capital dancer, I understand. We shall *see* if our styles suit. He is a fine young man and I like him very well.

Ah... ⸲cough⸳ ⸲cough⸳ ⸲cough⸳

Well, how do you like Mrs. Elton?

Not at all.

You are ungrateful.

What do you mean? No, don't tell me. Just tell me when we are to begin dancing. Come, let's ask my father.

We are unsure who should start the ball. We had hoped to ask Emma, but I believe Mrs. Elton will expect it. And she will think *Frank* ought to lead her.

I am an *engaged* man. That is...I promised the first dance to Miss Woodhouse.

Then *you* must lead Mrs. Elton out, my dear. You are the *host*, after all.

Emma submitted to being second to Mrs. Elton, though she had always considered the ball as peculiarly for her. It was almost enough to make one consider marrying--Mrs. Elton undoubtedly had gained the advantage, this time at least, in vanity completely gratified.

What a rare night this promises to be. Yet I am disturbed that Knightley does not dance. There he is among the standers-by, when he ought to be **dancing**.

Ah, he **smiles** as he catches my eye, but in general he looks so **grave**.

The ball proceeded pleasantly and everyone seemed happy...until the last dance before supper was to begin.

Do you not dance, Mr. Elton?

Most readily, Mrs. Weston, if you will partner me.

I am no dancer. But there is a young lady I should be very glad to see dancing-- Miss Smith.

Miss Smith! Oh! I had not observed. You are very obliging, but I am an old married man. My dancing days are over. If you will excuse me--

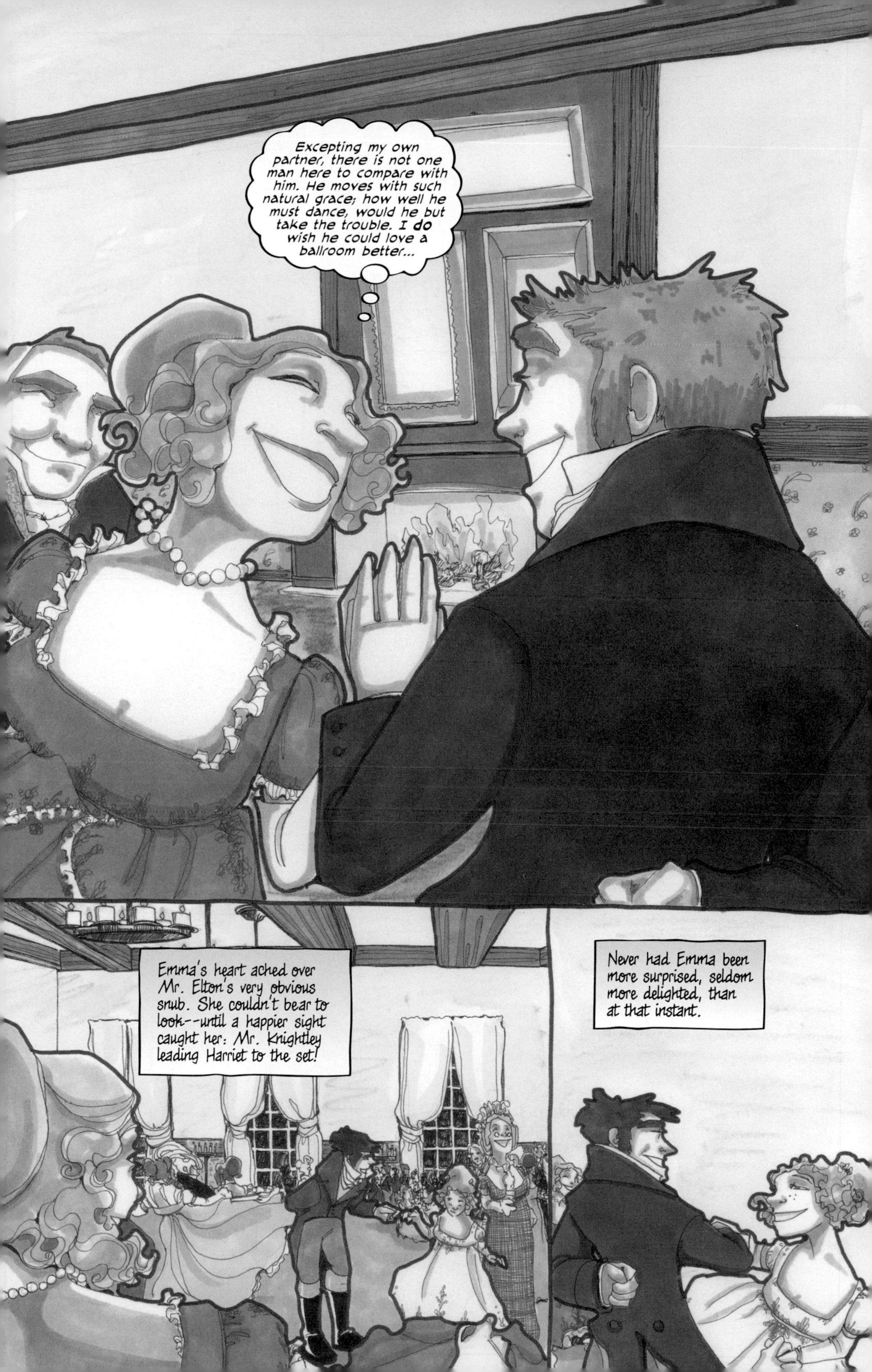
Excepting my own partner, there is not one man here to compare with him. He moves with such natural grace; how well he must dance, would he but take the trouble. I do wish he could love a ballroom better...
Emma's heart ached over Mr. Elton's very obvious snub. She couldn't bear to look--until a happier sight caught her: Mr. Knightley leading Harriet to the set!
Never had Emma been more surprised, seldom more delighted, than at that instant.

After supper, Emma had a chance to thank Mr. Knightley for his kindness.

The Eltons aimed at wounding *more* than Harriet. Why are they your enemies, Emma?

He wanted... that is, *I* wanted him to marry Harriet and they cannot forgive me.

Ah, look, Mr. Weston is calling for the next reel.

Whom shall you dance with?

With *you*, if you will ask me.

Will you indeed?

You have shown that you can dance, and we are not really so much brother and sister as to make it *improper*.

Brother and sister! No, indeed!

The following morning, just as Emma was congratulating herself on having achieved such a pleasant accord with Mr. Knightley regarding the Eltons--

Good *heavens!* What has happened?

From what I can tell, she was out walking beyond Mrs. Goddard's when she was set upon by a whole troop of young gypsies. I found her swooning on the road.

Oh, Mr. Churchill, *however* shall I thank you for saving me?

What did they do to you?

"It was so dreadful. I...I offered them a shilling, but they pressed me and clamored for my *whole purse.* It was...I was... o-o-oh!"

I'd heard the trampers were stealing chickens after dusk. But to accost a lady *in broad daylight!* I am only grateful the gates of Hartfield were so close by.

Even the coldest heart and steadiest brain can see how circumstance is at work to make them interesting to each other.

Emma's conjectures on the matter seemed quite justified when Harriet, now recovered from the attack, appeared at Hartfield a few days later.

I have brought these things, these tokens of Mr. Elton, to *burn* in your presence. I should have put them--and him--from my thoughts *long* ago.

Now in goes the court plaister I trimmed a length from when he cut his finger...and a pencil stub he discarded. Thank heavens, the *end* of Mr. Elton.

And when will be the beginning of *Mr. Churchill?*

Within a fortnight, Emma had her answer.

Whenever you marry, Harriet, I would advise you to keep goats as well as cows.

I will *never* marry.

Never marry! This is a new resolution. I hope it is not in compliment to Mr. Elton.

Oh! No...! There are others far *superior* to Mr. Elton.

I won't pretend to misunderstand you. I take it that your resolution to never marry stems from the notion that this person whom you esteem is too much your *superior* to think of you.

Indeed, I am not so mad. It is a pleasure to admire him from a distance.

I am not surprised. The *service* he rendered you surely warmed your heart.

The very recollection of it... his *noble* look, my *wretchedness* before. Such a change in one minute--from *perfect misery* to *perfect happiness.*

We were very *wrong* before, and must be *cautious* now. Let no names pass our lips. I am determined against all interference, so will only say one thing--let *his* behavior guide your senses.

He is your *superior*, no doubt, and there are obstacles of a serious nature. Yet more wonderful things have taken place, and there have been matches of much *greater* disparity.

One bright June afternoon, as Mr. Knightley made his way toward Hartfield, he fell in with a large party, also bound for the same destination.

Harriet and I met up with this merry group in Highbury and I have invited them all to drink tea with Papa.

Oh, look, it's Mr. Perry. By the by, what ever happened to his plan of setting up his own carriage, Mrs. Weston? I am sure you wrote me about it several months ago.

Me? *Impossible, Frank!* I did not know he had such a plan.

I was sure you mentioned it. Perhaps I *dreamt* it. I dream of *everybody* at Highbury when I am away from here--apparently even the Perrys.

To own the truth, there was such a plan this spring. Mrs. Perry *was* anxious that he should have a carriage and came to tell my mother--in confidence--of her scheme.

Jane, don't you recall her visit? I never mentioned it to a soul, for I know I am a talker and things do pop out. I wish I were like Jane. *She* never betrays the least thing in the world.

Once the tea was served, several in the group decided to play at anagrams with Emma's childhood alphabet blocks.

Here is one--

"Blunder!" It spells "blunder."

What do you think?

Nonsense! For shame!

I will give it to her. Shall I?

No, you must not.

But Mr. Churchill would not be stayed...

I did not think proper names were allowed.

I was going to say the same thing. It is time for us to be going, before the evening closes in. We must wish you all a good night.

Once the other guests had left, Mr. Knightley accosted Emma in the library.

Pray, Emma, in what lay the great *amusement*, the poignant *sting* of the last word given to you and Miss Fairfax?

I saw the word and am curious to know how it could be so very *entertaining* to the one and so very *distressing* to the other.

It meant nothing at all. A mere *joke* among ourselves.

A joke confined to you and Mr. Churchill.

Emma made no answer, but busied herself with arranging some books upon a small table.

My dear girl, do you think you perfectly understand the degree of acquaintance between the gentleman and that lady?

Between Mr. Churchill and Miss Fairfax? Oh, yes, *perfectly.* Why do you make a doubt of it?

Have you never had reason to think he admired her or that she admired him?

Never! Not for the twentieth part of a moment did such an idea occur to me. How could such a thing enter *your* head?

I have lately imagined seeing symptoms of *attachment* between them, certain expressive *looks*, which I don't believe they meant to be public.

Oh! You amuse me excessively. I am delighted to discover that you actually can allow your imagination to wander. But I am sorry to check that first essay--there is *no* admiration between them, I do assure you.

I am convinced the appearances that struck you have arisen from a peculiar set of circumstances and feelings of a totally different nature. While I *presume* it to be so on her side, I can answer for the gentleman that there is only indifference on his side.

The confidence of her reply both staggered and silenced Mr. Knightley.

Emma was in gay spirits and would have prolonged Mr. Knightley's visit...but his feelings were too *irritated* for talking.

That he might not be irritated into an absolute fever by Mr. Woodhouse's habitually blazing fire, he soon afterwards took a hasty leave and walked home to the coolness and solitude of Donwell Abbey.

With summer fully arrived, it was natural that Emma's nearest neighbors should plan an outing to Box Hill, the local scenic vista.

You could explore Donwell Abbey. That may be done without horses. Come and eat my strawberries. They are ripening fast.

Sadly, Miss, the wheeler is gone lame.

This is most vexatious. I was hoping to assess Box Hill as a possible destination for when the Sucklings arrive in the fall. These delays and disappointments are so odious.

I should like that excessively, Mr. Knightley! I believe we all should.

Ah...um... Just allow me a week to prepare my housekeeper.

Very well, a week then and we shall descend upon your strawberry beds. A pity I cannot arrive by donkey, with my *caro sposo* walking beside me. It would be quite the thing.

You may arrive however you wish, Mrs. Elton. I desire everything to be to your taste.

I am sure you do. Under that peculiar dry, blunt manner, I know you have the warmest heart.

In the meantime, the invitation was also extended to Mr. Woodhouse and the Highbury ladies. By the time the designated day arrived, the lame horse had recovered--Mr. Woodhouse was carried to the Abbey in his own carriage--and it was decided to revive the Box Hill trip for the following morning.

I thought Mr. Churchill had been among those invited.

He wrote that he had been delayed a trifle this morning. He will ride directly to the Abbey when he does not find us at Hartfield.

Once Mr. Woodhouse was settled in a small parlor with a good fire...

...Emma and the other guests set out to tour the house and grounds. She had not been there in a great while and so was eager to refresh her memory.

It is a rambling, irregular place, larger than Hartfield and so different. Yet it is just as it should be...

Some faults of temper John Knightley may have, but Isabella has connected herself unexceptionably. She has given our family neither men, nor names, nor places that could raise a blush.

Miss Woodhouse! Do come join us. The strawberries are at their peak!

The best fruit in England-- Everybody's favorite--

Always wholesome-- These are the finest beds--

Delightful to gather for one's self--

The only way of really enjoying them.

Morning decidedly the best time-- I could cry over the price of strawberries in London--

At Maple Grove, the cultivation beds are to be renewed--

Delicious fruit--inferior to cherries--

Only objection to gathering strawberries is the stooping--the glaring sun--I am tired to death--must go and sit in the shade.

Once the three had settled under a broad tree, Emma was obliged to overhear Mrs. Elton's plans for Jane's future.

...It is a most desirable situation. Not with Mrs. Bragge, alas, but with her cousin, who is an acquaintance of my sister and is known at Maple Grove.

I heard from the woman only this morning and she awaits your response.

I have told you in the clearest terms, I do not intend to seek any employment at present.

Nonsense. It won't do to whistle this sort of offer down the wind. With your leave, I shall write to her this very evening expressing your grateful acceptance.

Please, do not. I...I don't know what else to say to convince you that I have no wish to change my situation.

My dear Miss Fairfax, you must trust *me* to know what is best for you.

It is astonishing to me how Jane can bear this at all. I have never seen her appear so vexed.

There he is... with Miss Smith, on that hill overlooking Abbey Mill Farm. Let us join them.

Should we not walk? Let us seek out Mr. Knightley to escort us through his park.

An odd tete-a-tete, but I am glad to see it. There was a time he would have scorned her as a companion.

This is a sweet view. English verdure and English culture seen under a bright sun.

I have been giving Miss Smith some lessons in agriculture. And she has been bearing up very well under the onslaught.

I should not become alarmed that Harriet is gazing so soulfully at the Martin farm. Robert Martin has no doubt forgotten her and she him.

Ladies, perhaps you would care to take a few turns around the Elizabethan knot garden with me.

We would be delighted.

I am most uneasy over Frank's absence. I wish he would sell that wild-eyed black mare, for I do not trust her.

Everyone soon gathered inside to enjoy a cold repast.

Make sure of it, my dear...Mrs. Churchill has merely suffered another of her attacks and required him to attend her.

After the meal, Emma elected to remain indoors with her father while the other guests went to tour the fishponds. Her father had just begun to display the Abbey's treasures to her, when an agitated Miss Fairfax appeared at the door.

Oh...I'm sorry to disturb you, Miss Woodhouse, but I need to speak to you.

What ever is the matter?

I am going home. My aunt is not aware how long we have been absent, and I am determined to go there directly. Please let her know when she comes in.

Then let me order our carriage for you. It is very hot and you are already fatigued.

Yes, I am fatigued, but it is not the sort that you think. A brisk walk will refresh me. We...we all know how it is to be worried in spirit, and my spirits exhaust me. The greatest kindness you can show me is to let me have my own way.

Of course. Whatever you require.

Oh, Miss Woodhouse, the comfort of being sometimes alone!

Such a home, indeed! Such an aunt! I do pity you. And the more sensibility you betray of their horrors, the more I shall like you.

Emma had barely resumed her place at her father's side, when Frank Churchill appeared.

Ah, Mr. Churchill! Mrs. Weston will be greatly relieved to see you in one piece. She feared your black mare had thrown you into a hedge.

It was my aunt caused the delay--she suffered a mild seizure and I could not get away till very late. I hurried that mare as best I could, but it was hellish.

I probably should not have come at all. The heat was excessive and I have never suffered anything like it.

You will be cooler if you sit down.

I should probably just go back to Richmond.

The party will be breaking up. I met one departing guest as I arrived. Madness in such heat. Absolute madness!

Perhaps if you take some cold refreshment... something to cool your humor.

No, nothing. Well, maybe some spruce beer, then, before I set off for home.

I am glad I have done being in love with him. I should not like a man who is so discomposed by a hot day. Harriet's easy, sweet temper will not mind it so much.

Mr. Churchill grew more composed after a time...

Once my aunt is well, I shall go abroad. I shall never be easy until I have seen these distant places.

Your aunt and uncle would never allow you to leave England.

Perhaps they will go too. A warm climate might be good for my aunt's health. I tell you, I feel a strong persuasion today that I shall soon be abroad. I am sick of England and would leave tomorrow if I could.

You are sick of prosperity and indulgence. Invent a few hardships and be content to stay.

You are quite mistaken. I am thwarted in everything material. I do not consider myself a fortunate person.

You are in better spirits than when you first arrived. Food and drink clearly revive you.

We are taking a picnic to Box Hill tomorrow-- you will join us. It's not Switzerland, but fine for a man in need of change. Will you stay tonight?

Nay, I will go home in the cool of the evening.

And come again in the cool of the morning? No? Then pray stay at Richmond.

That will make me crosser still. I can't bear to think of you all here without me.

These are difficulties you must settle for yourself. Choose your own degree of crossness.

Well...if you wish me to join the party, then I will.

The following morning, a lively group set out for Box Hill--

Box Hill, the summit of the North Downs in Surrey, lay but seven miles from Highbury, yet Emma had never seen it. She determined to walk at once to the top and enlisted Mr. Churchill and Harriet to join her.

Alas, when they rejoined the main group, it had broken up into smaller parties and Mr. Weston could not make them harmonize.

I have never seen Mr. Churchill so silent or stupid. And while he is so dull, it is no wonder Harriet is dull as well. They are both insufferable today.

When they all sat down together for lunch, Mr. Churchill at last grew talkative and gay.

Thank you for telling me to come today. I could wish I were always under your command... especially when my own self command deserts me.

My command only dates from three o'clock yesterday.

Truly? And yet I first saw you in February.

Your gallantry is unanswerable.

But, look--nobody speaks but ourselves and you are talking rather too much nonsense for seven silent people.

Our companions are excessively stupid. What shall we do to rouse them?

Ladies and gentlemen... Miss Woodhouse--who presides wherever she may be--has given me a commission. She desires to know what you are thinking.

Is she really sure she desires that?

No, no! That is the last thing I would stand the brunt of right now.

That is the sort of thing even I--as a married lady--would not think myself privileged to inquire into.

Quite so, my love. Some ladies say anything. Best to pass it off as a joke.

Miss Woodhouse waives her right of knowing what you might be thinking and asks only to be entertained by each of you. She demands either one thing very clever, two things moderately clever or three things very dull indeed.

Oh, then I not need be uneasy. 'Three things very dull indeed.' That will do for me. I shall be sure to say three dull things as soon as I open my mouth, shan't I?

Ah, Miss Bates, there may be a difficulty. You will be limited as to number--only three at once--

Ah, to be sure. I see what she means and will try to hold my tongue. I must make myself very disagreeable else she would not have said such a thing to an old friend.

Mr. Weston broke the tension with a conundrum of his own devising.

What two letters of the alphabet express perfection? You will never guess, so I will tell you: M. A.

Emma... Do you understand?

Not the most *perfect* perfection today, alas.

The Eltons wanted no part of the games and soon took themselves off for a stroll.

Lucky couple to suit each other so well after marrying as they did upon an acquaintance formed only at a public place.

As for any real knowledge of a person's disposition that Bath--or any public place--can give, it is all nothing.

It is only by seeing a woman in her home, among her own set, that you can make any judgment.

How many a man has committed himself on short notice and rued it the rest of his life?

While it's true such imprudent attachments do arise, I believe only weak, irresolute characters would suffer an unfortunate acquaintance to be an oppression or inconvenience forever.

I defer to you, Miss Fairfax.

I have so little confidence in my own judgment, I hope that someone will choose a wife for me. Will you, Miss Woodhouse? Adopt her, educate her, make her like yourself.

If I undertake the commission, you shall have a charming wife.

Don't forget now. I shall be abroad and when I return, I shall come to you for a wife.

Aunt, shall we join the Eltons? Mrs. Elton appears to be waving to me.

As the picnic broke up, Mr. Knightley sought out Emma for a private word.

Emma, I must once more speak to you as I have been used to do, a privilege endured rather than allowed. I cannot see you acting wrong without a remonstrance.

How could you be so unfeeling to Miss Bates? So insolent in your wit, to a woman of her character, age, and situation?

I had not thought it possible.

How could I *help* saying it? It was not so very bad and I daresay she didn't understand it.

I assure you she did. She took your *full* meaning. She has talked of it since, wondering at your own and your father's generosity and attention to her if you found her so irksome.

Oh, there is not a better creature in the world. But you must allow that the good and the ridiculous are most unfortunately blended in her.

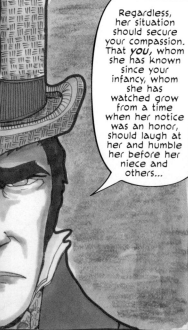

Regardless, her situation should secure your compassion. That *you*, whom she has known since your infancy, whom she has watched grow from a time when her notice was an honor, should laugh at her and humble her before her niece and others...

It was *badly done,* Emma. Badly done, indeed.

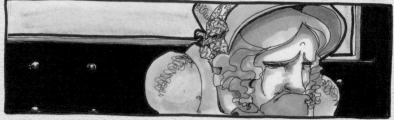

As Emma reflected that evening on the wretchedness of the trip to Box Hill, she felt it was more to be abhorred than any outing in her recollection. She must do something to make amends--and quickly.

As a daughter, I hope no one can reproach my behavior to my father. Ah, but as a friend to Miss Bates, I have so often been remiss--and even scornful.

She determined to visit Miss Bates the very next morning.

Perhaps I will meet Mr. Knightley in Highbury. I am not ashamed that he should know of my penitence.

Ah, Miss Woodhouse. How kind. But I suppose you have heard the news and have come to wish us joy...

Joy, ma'am?

Though it does not seem like joy to us. How we shall miss our Jane. Such long letters she's written to Colonel Campbell and Mrs. Dixon...and with tears in her eyes the whole time.

Alas, I have just sent her to bed with a severe headache.

She has taken a position then?

Yes, with a Mrs. Smallridge, who has three delightful children and resides quite near Maple Grove. Of course Mrs. Elton arranged it.

Jane took all evening to think it over and I believe it was directly after we heard from Mr. Elton that Mr. Churchill had been called to Richmond by his aunt that Jane finally decided.

I see you are staring at her pianoforte. Dear Jane was speaking to it only minutes ago--"You and I must part" she said.

Please, let her know I am thinking of her and send her *all* my good wishes.

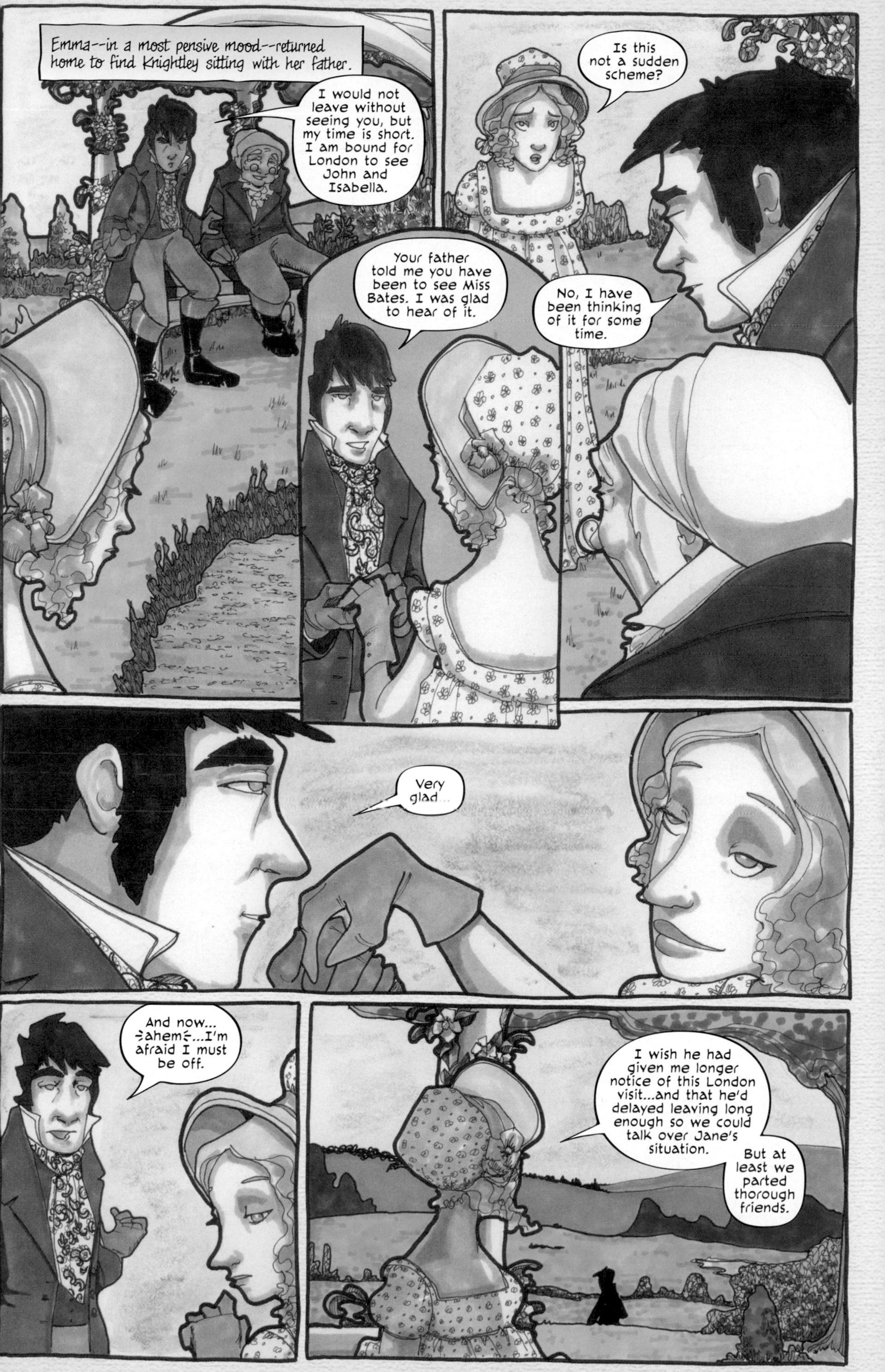
Emma--in a most pensive mood--returned home to find Knightley sitting with her father.
I would not leave without seeing you, but my time is short. I am bound for London to see John and Isabella.
Is this not a sudden scheme?
No, I have been thinking of it for some time.
Your father told me you have been to see Miss Bates. I was glad to hear of it.
Very glad...
And now... ahem...I'm afraid I must be off.
I wish he had given me longer notice of this London visit...and that he'd delayed leaving long enough so we could talk over Jane's situation.
But at least we parted thorough friends.

Mr. Knightley had scarcely been gone a day when a message was sent from Richmond to Randalls--Mrs. Churchill had died of a seizure! After being disliked for twenty-five years, the woman was finally spoken of with compassionate allowances.

Poor creature. No doubt she was in greater pain than anyone supposed. Such continual discomfort would try anyone's temper. How grief-struck her husband must be.

And how freed, how benefited now is Frank Churchill. Answerable only to an uncle whom no one fears. If Frank desires an attachment to Harriet, he shall meet no obstacle.

Yet Harriet seemed unconcerned when she learned that Frank's familial obligations to his uncle would keep him from Highbury for a time.

Mr. Churchill writes that they will be visiting with his uncle's friend in Windsor for a week.

I daresay they are both happy to be making their own decisions for a change.

So while it seemed Harriet's prospects were opening up, Jane Fairfax's were closing as the date of her employment grew near. Emma made several attempts to see her, but was turned away.

You are very kind...and my niece is most thankful for the arrowroot jelly you sent, but except for Mrs. Elton, Jane is too unwell for visitors.

With so many perplexing things going on around her, Emma was almost cross when Mr. Weston arrived with a cryptic message.

Can you come to Randalls this morning? Mrs. Weston must see you...alone.

Is she unwell?

No, just a bit agitated.

It is impossible to refuse when you ask in such a way. But whatever is the matter?

Please, you must not press me. You will know it all soon enough.

Upon arriving at Randalls, Mr. Weston took himself off and left Emma in his wife's care.

What is it my dear friend? Something of an unpleasant nature?

It relates to Frank Churchill. He...he has been here this morning on a most extraordinary errand. To tell us of his secret engagement to Jane Fairfax.

Jane Fairfax! Good God! You are not serious? You do not mean it?

There has been an arrangement between them since they met at Weymouth in October. No one, not a soul, knew of it.

This has hurt me very much, Emma, and his father equally. Some part of his conduct we cannot excuse.

I will not pretend to misunderstand. And to give you all the relief in my power, be assured that you need not fear for me-- I was not harmed by his attentions.

Oh, I admit I was at first attached to him...and how it came to cease is perhaps the wonder. Truly, I have cared nothing about him for at least three months.

Hearing you say that has done me much good.

But that does not excuse him. What right had he to distinguish one young woman with marked attention when he belonged to another? How could he tell who else he might be hurting? How could she bear it, looking on while he flirted shamelessly with me?

There were misunderstandings between them. He made that very clear the short time he was here.

He was not aware that Miss Fairfax had taken a position or that she was so unwell--but I believe they have ironed it out.

Well, I suppose I wish them happy. But it has been an abominable sort of proceeding.

Emma fretted most for Harriet--now twice disappointed in love, but when next they met, Harriet was calm and collected.

Is not this the oddest news that ever was? I mean about Mr. Churchill and Jane Fairfax being secretly betrothed.

I never had the slightest notion, otherwise I would have cautioned you, Harriet.

Why me? You do not think I care about Mr. Churchill.

Your feelings may have altered, but not long ago you confided to me--

And spoke no names, at your request. Though when I spoke of his vast superiority, I was sure you guessed, having known him your whole life.

... Harriet, are you speaking of--Mr. Knightley?

To be sure I am. Who else rendered me such a singular service?

I thought you meant Frank Churchill... er...protecting you from the gypsies.

No, it was the far more precious circumstance of Mr. Knightley asking me to dance when Mr. Elton shunned me.

And I encouraged your feelings. Good God! This has been a most unfortunate mistake? What is to be done?

You may imagine him five hundred million times above me, yet you yourself said stranger matches have happened. He may not mind the disparity.

I hope, dear Miss Woodhouse, you will not set yourself against it. But you are too good for that, I am sure.

Have you any notion that he returns your affection?

Yes. Yes, I must say that I have.

The instant Harriet left, the truth of Emma's own emotions regarding Mr. Knightley struck her like a blow.

Oh, God! That I had never seen her! That I had never brought her forward to his notice.

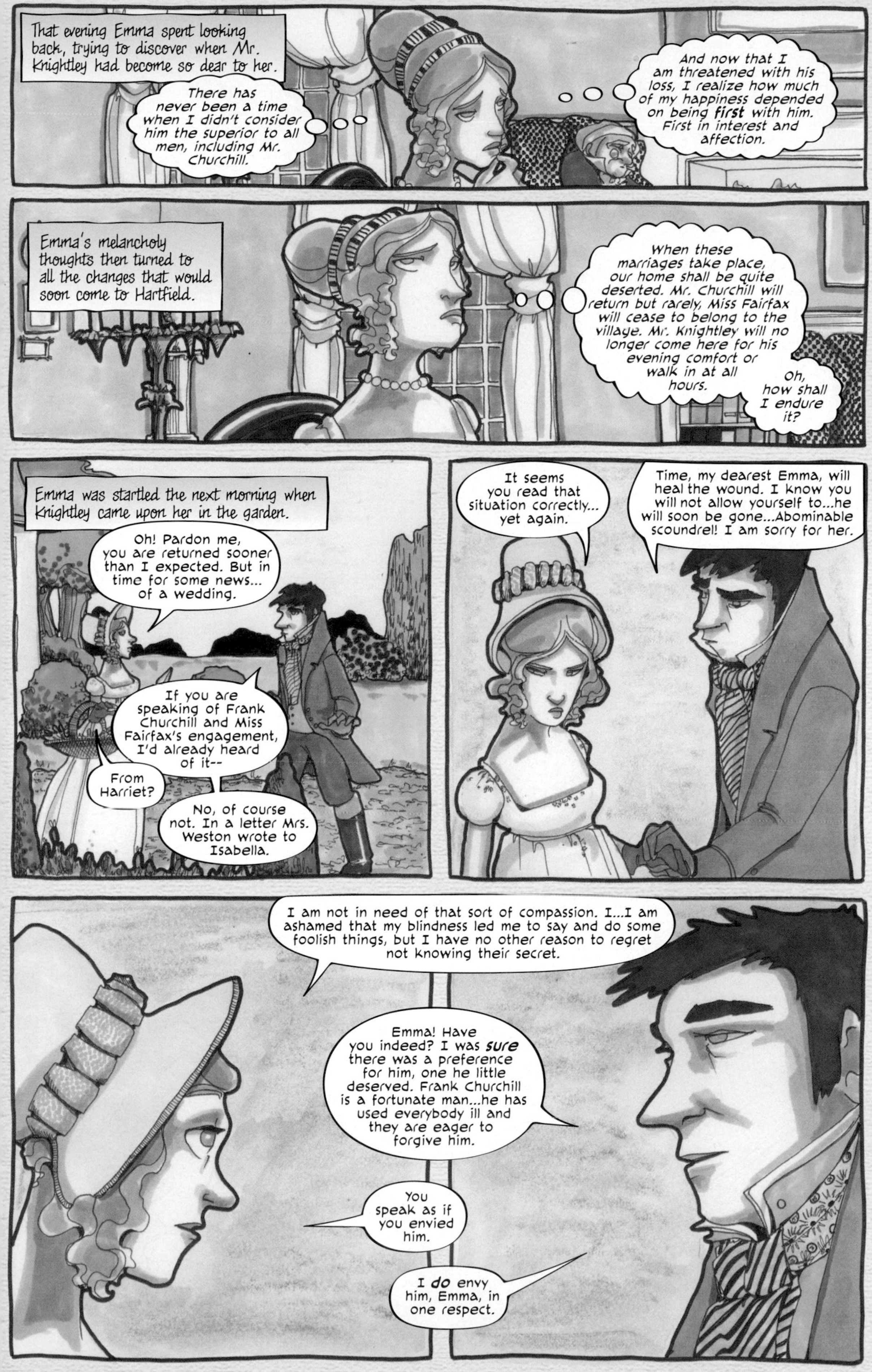
That evening Emma spent looking back, trying to discover when Mr. Knightley had become so dear to her.
There has never been a time when I didn't consider him the superior to all men, including Mr. Churchill.
And now that I am threatened with his loss, I realize how much of my happiness depended on being **first** with him. First in interest and affection.
Emma's melancholy thoughts then turned to all the changes that would soon come to Hartfield.
When these marriages take place, our home shall be quite deserted. Mr. Churchill will return but rarely, Miss Fairfax will cease to belong to the village. Mr. Knightley will no longer come here for his evening comfort or walk in at all hours.
Oh, how shall I endure it?
Emma was startled the next morning when Knightley came upon her in the garden.
Oh! Pardon me, you are returned sooner than I expected. But in time for some news... of a wedding.
If you are speaking of Frank Churchill and Miss Fairfax's engagement, I'd already heard of it--
From Harriet?
No, of course not. In a letter Mrs. Weston wrote to Isabella.
It seems you read that situation correctly... yet again.
Time, my dearest Emma, will heal the wound. I know you will not allow yourself to...he will soon be gone...Abominable scoundrel! I am sorry for her.
I am not in need of that sort of compassion. I...I am ashamed that my blindness led me to say and do some foolish things, but I have no other reason to regret not knowing their secret.
Emma! Have you indeed? I was ***sure*** there was a preference for him, one he little deserved. Frank Churchill is a fortunate man...he has used everybody ill and they are eager to forgive him.
You speak as if you envied him.
I ***do*** envy him, Emma, in one respect.

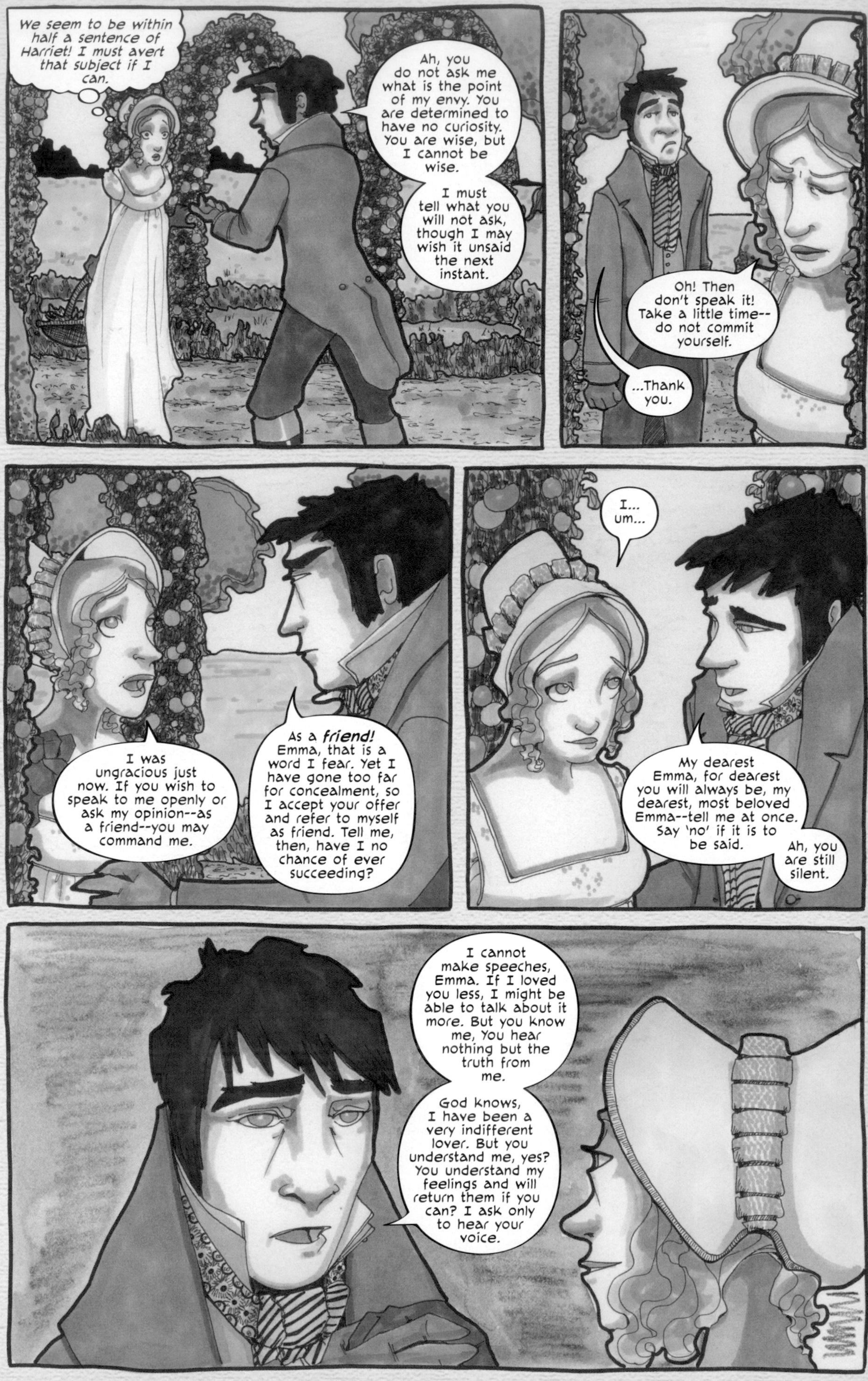
We seem to be within half a sentence of Harriet! I must avert that subject if I can.
Ah, you do not ask me what is the point of my envy. You are determined to have no curiosity. You are wise, but I cannot be wise.
I must tell what you will not ask, though I may wish it unsaid the next instant.
Oh! Then don't speak it! Take a little time-- do not commit yourself.
...Thank you.
I was ungracious just now. If you wish to speak to me openly or ask my opinion--as a friend--you may command me.
As a friend! Emma, that is a word I fear. Yet I have gone too far for concealment, so I accept your offer and refer to myself as friend. Tell me, then, have I no chance of ever succeeding?
I... um...
My dearest Emma, for dearest you will always be, my dearest, most beloved Emma--tell me at once. Say 'no' if it is to be said.
Ah, you are still silent.
I cannot make speeches, Emma. If I loved you less, I might be able to talk about it more. But you know me, You hear nothing but the truth from me.
God knows, I have been a very indifferent lover. But you understand me, yes? You understand my feelings and will return them if you can? I ask only to hear your voice.

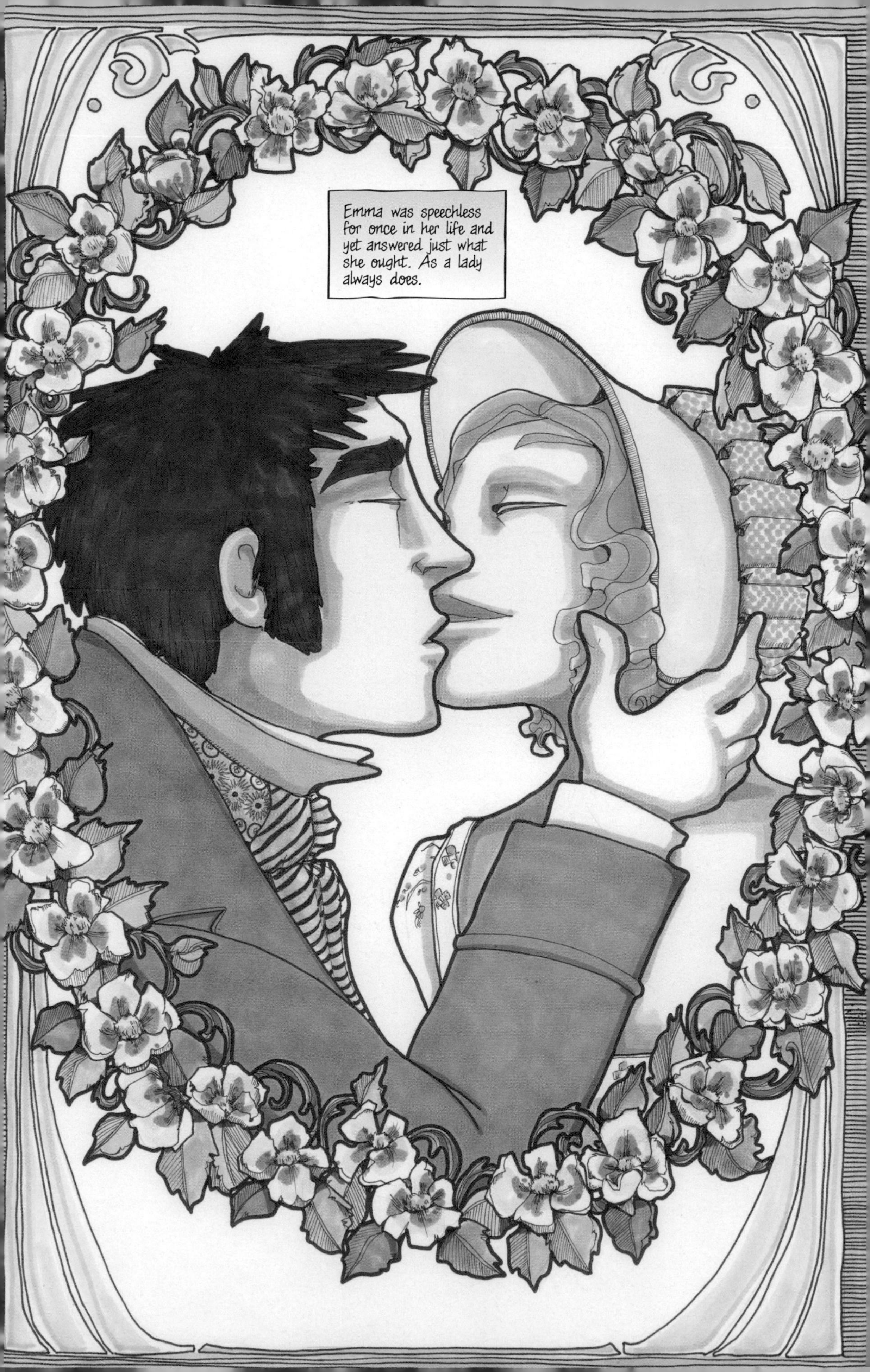
Emma was speechless for once in her life and yet answered just what she ought. As a lady always does.

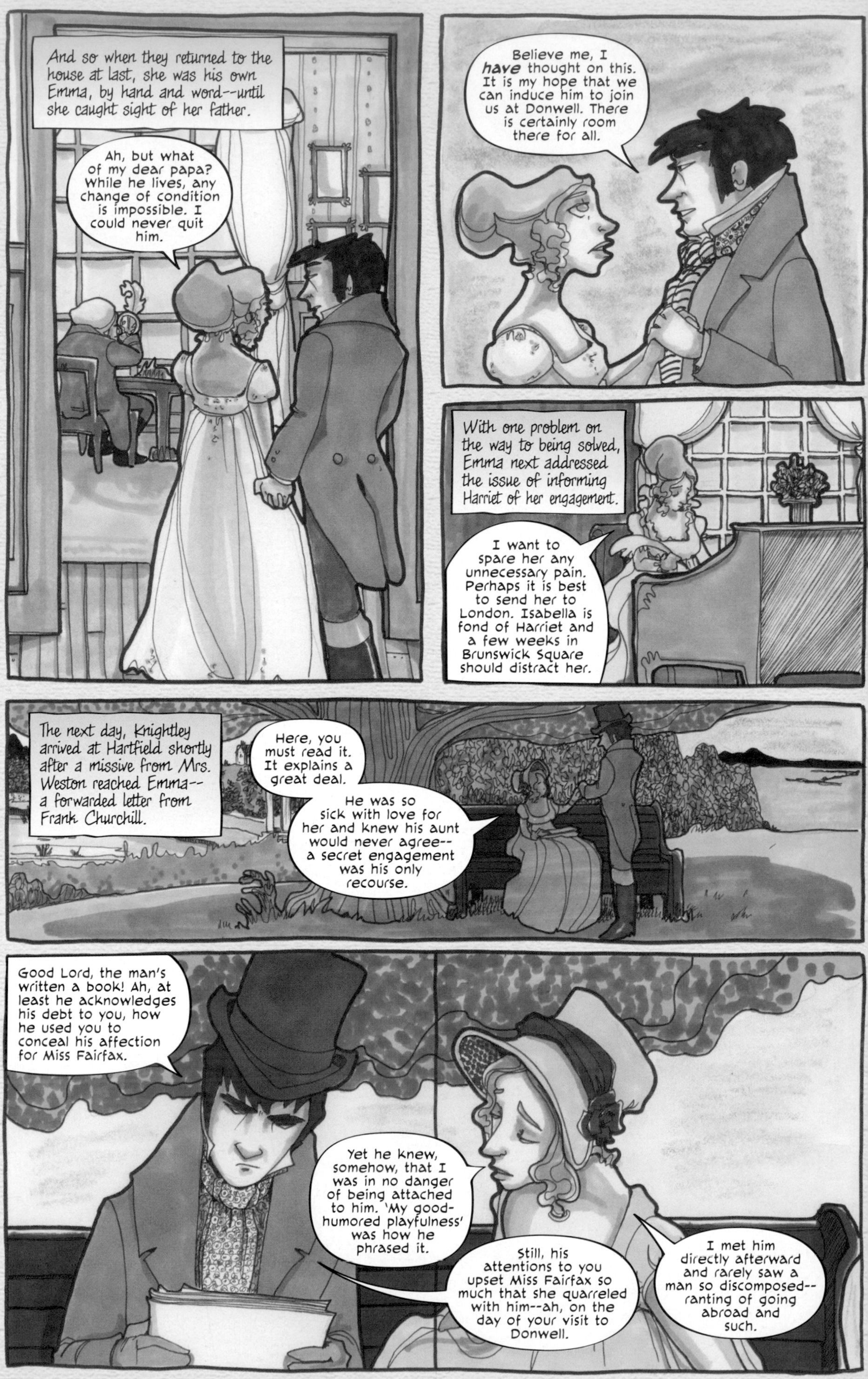

And so when they returned to the house at last, she was his own Emma, by hand and word--until she caught sight of her father.
Ah, but what of my dear papa? While he lives, any change of condition is impossible. I could never quit him.
Believe me, I have thought on this. It is my hope that we can induce him to join us at Donwell. There is certainly room there for all.
With one problem on the way to being solved, Emma next addressed the issue of informing Harriet of her engagement.
I want to spare her any unnecessary pain. Perhaps it is best to send her to London. Isabella is fond of Harriet and a few weeks in Brunswick Square should distract her.
The next day, Knightley arrived at Hartfield shortly after a missive from Mrs. Weston reached Emma--a forwarded letter from Frank Churchill.
Here, you must read it. It explains a great deal.
He was so sick with love for her and knew his aunt would never agree--a secret engagement was his only recourse.
Good Lord, the man's written a book! Ah, at least he acknowledges his debt to you, how he used you to conceal his affection for Miss Fairfax.
Yet he knew, somehow, that I was in no danger of being attached to him. 'My good-humored playfulness' was how he phrased it.
Still, his attentions to you upset Miss Fairfax so much that she quarreled with him--ah, on the day of your visit to Donwell.
I met him directly afterward and rarely saw a man so discomposed--ranting of going abroad and such.

"Blameless, he calls her now and I agree, though he thought her cold at the time. So she broke off the engagement--the very morning of his aunt's death."

"I can pity him for that unfortunate timing. He at once wrote a note to reassure her but in the confusion of the sad day, neglected to send it."

"She then returned all his letters and advised him to send any future correspondence to Mrs. Smallbridge. Quite a blow, as he did not know she had taken a position as governess."

"Bravo, Miss F! Resolute to the last."

"And so he immediately sought out his uncle and vouchsafed his sanction to wed her. And came at last to Highbury with a proper proposal for his lady."

"He says he is "luckier than he deserves" that she took him back. At least he and I are in agreement there."

"You may reserve judgment, but I think the better of him for opening his heart to Mrs. Weston."

"Ever since I left you yesterday, my mind has been at work on one problem. I fear a transplant to Donwell would risk your father's comfort or even his health."

"So now I am considering coming to Hartfield, should it please you. If this continues to be your home, it must be mine as well."

"Your bailiff, Mr. Larkin, will not like it. You must get his consent before you ask mine. But I believe the idea will grow on me over time."

"I should be completely happy, save for Harriet. How sad that my blessing must advance her suffering. In time, knightley will be forgotten and even supplanted in her affection. But not soon, I fear. It is too much to hope--even of Harriet--that she could be in love with more than *three* men in one year."

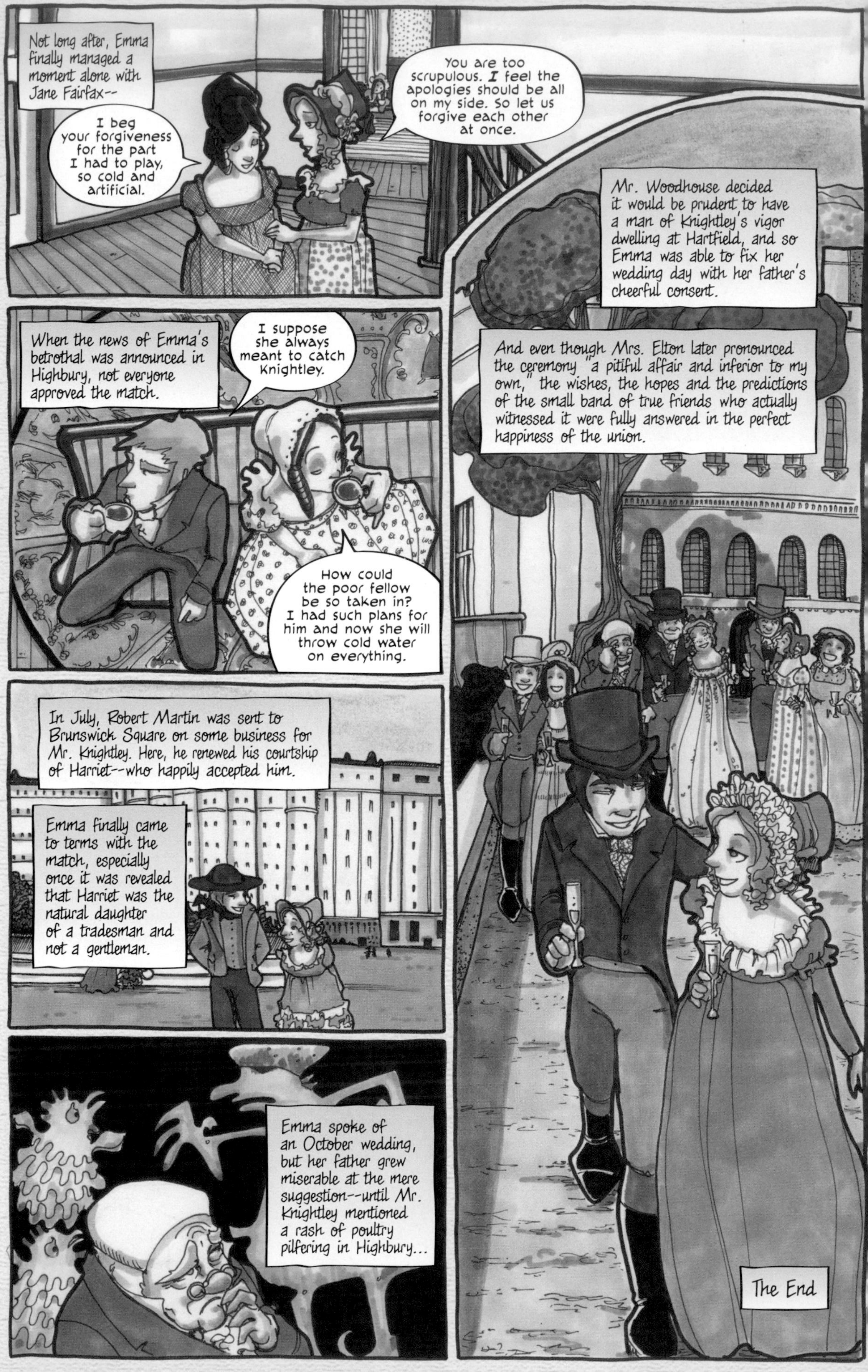

Not long after, Emma finally managed a moment alone with Jane Fairfax--
I beg your forgiveness for the part I had to play, so cold and artificial.
You are too scrupulous. I feel the apologies should be all on my side. So let us forgive each other at once.
When the news of Emma's betrothal was announced in Highbury, not everyone approved the match.
I suppose she always meant to catch Knightley.
How could the poor fellow be so taken in? I had such plans for him and now she will throw cold water on everything.
In July, Robert Martin was sent to Brunswick Square on some business for Mr. Knightley. Here, he renewed his courtship of Harriet--who happily accepted him.
Emma finally came to terms with the match, especially once it was revealed that Harriet was the natural daughter of a tradesman and not a gentleman.
Emma spoke of an October wedding, but her father grew miserable at the mere suggestion--until Mr. Knightley mentioned a rash of poultry pilfering in Highbury...
Mr. Woodhouse decided it would be prudent to have a man of Knightley's vigor dwelling at Hartfield, and so Emma was able to fix her wedding day with her father's cheerful consent.
And even though Mrs. Elton later pronounced the ceremony "a pitiful affair and inferior to my own," the wishes, the hopes and the predictions of the small band of true friends who actually witnessed it were fully answered in the perfect happiness of the union.
The End

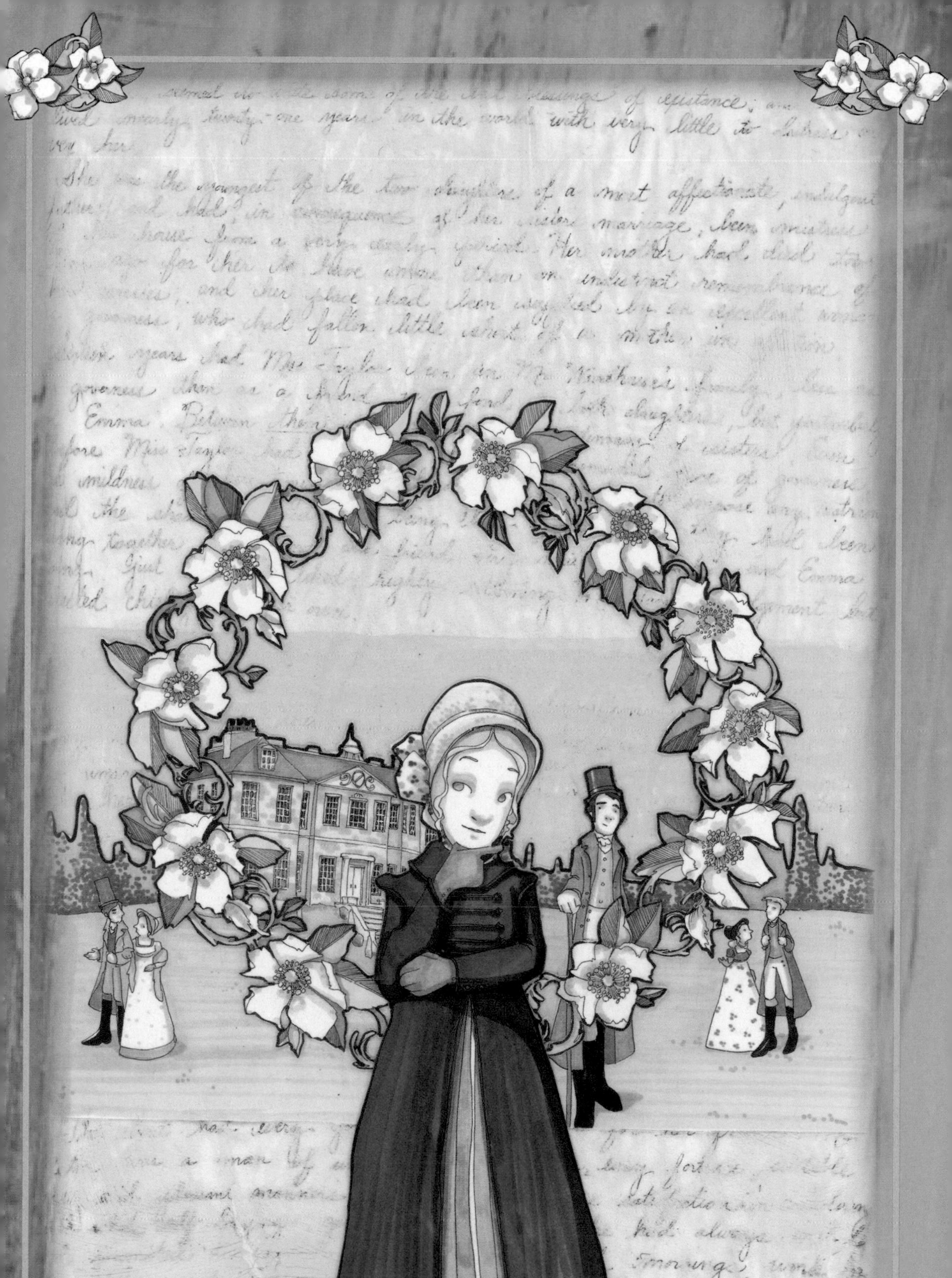
lived nearly twenty-one years in the world with very little to distress or vex her.
She was the youngest of the two daughters of a most affectionate, indulgent

One

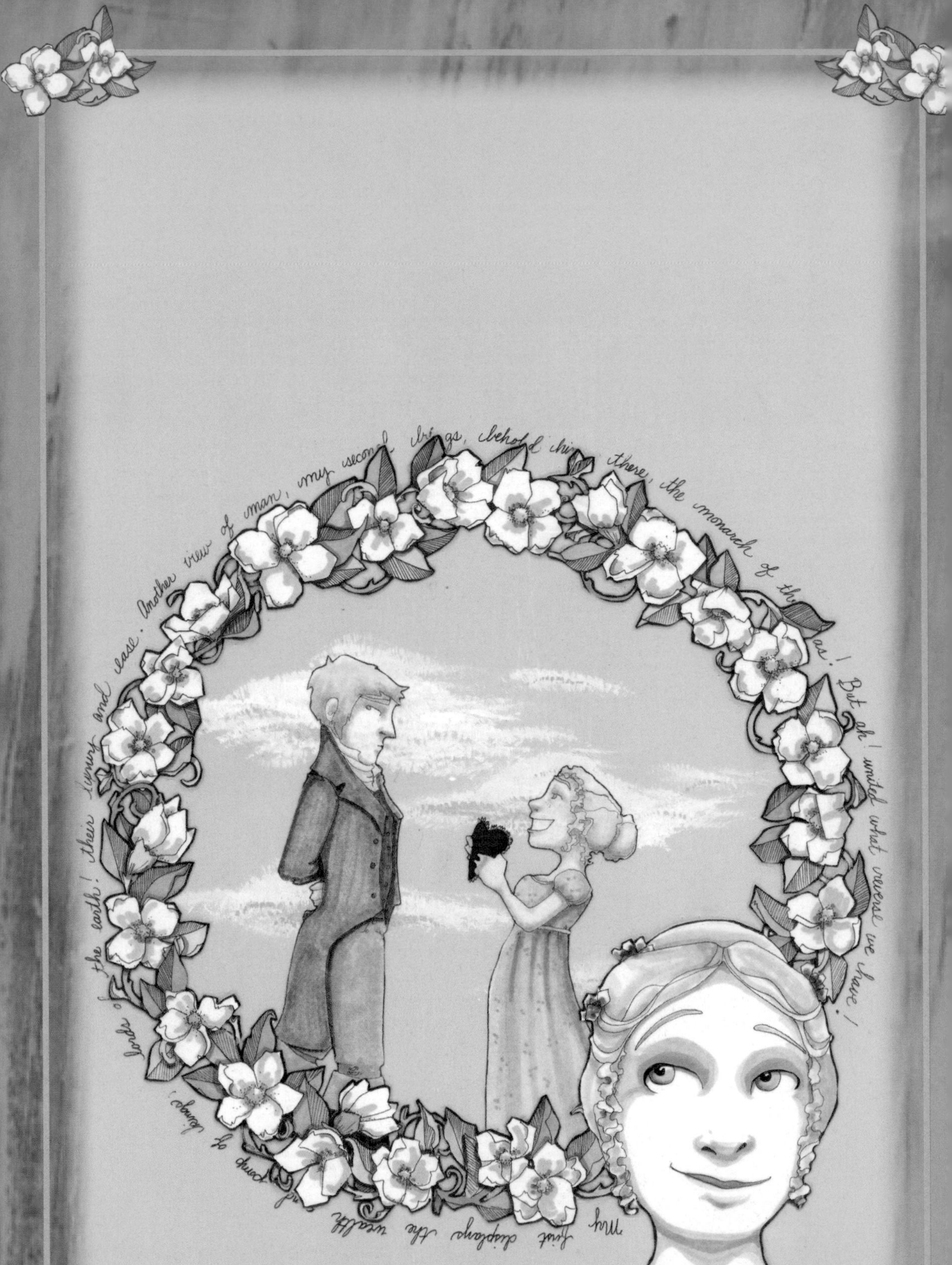
Another view of man, my second
the monarch of
But ah! united what reverse we have!
My first displays the wealth
pomp of kings,
the earth! their luxury and ease.

Two

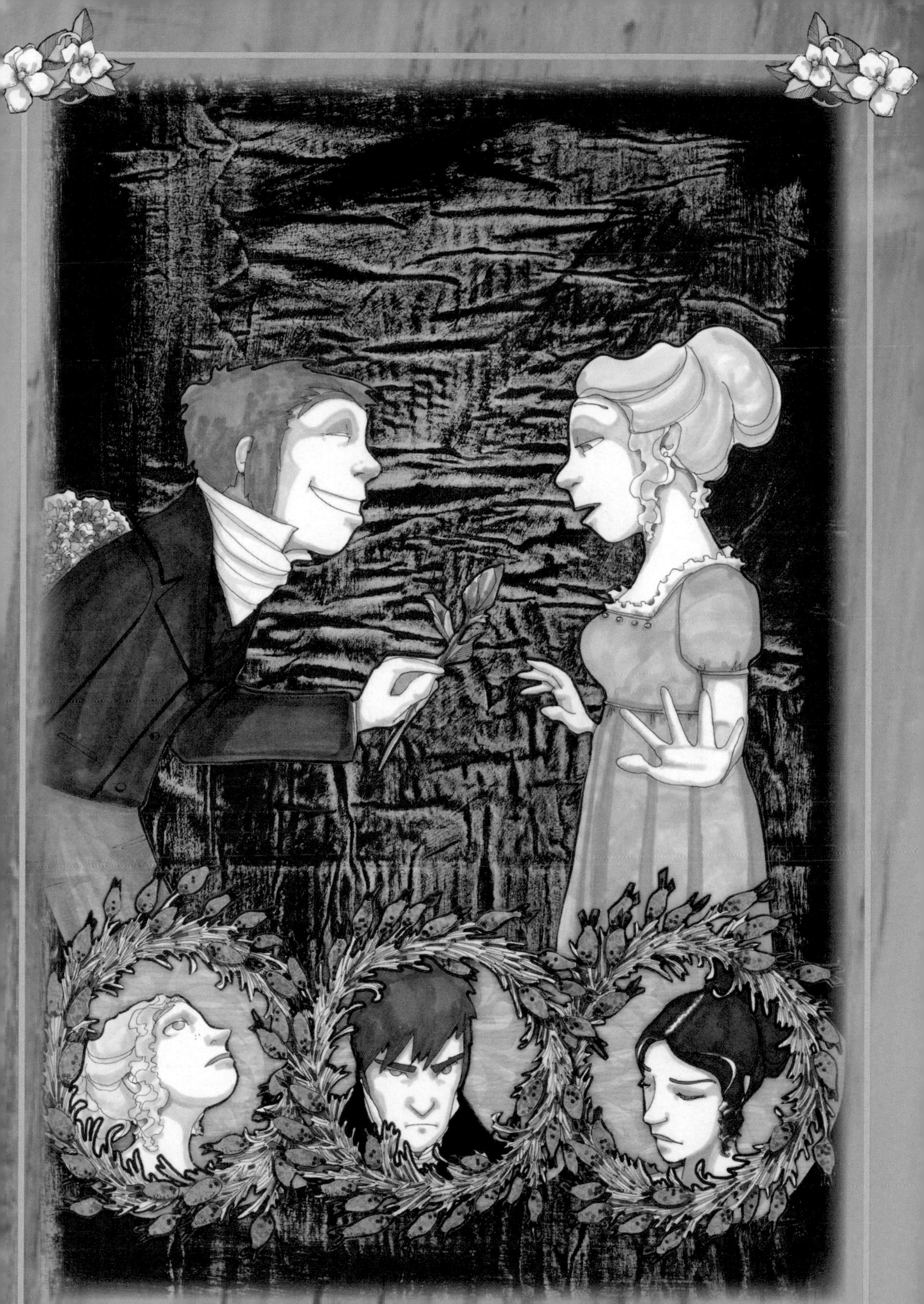

Three

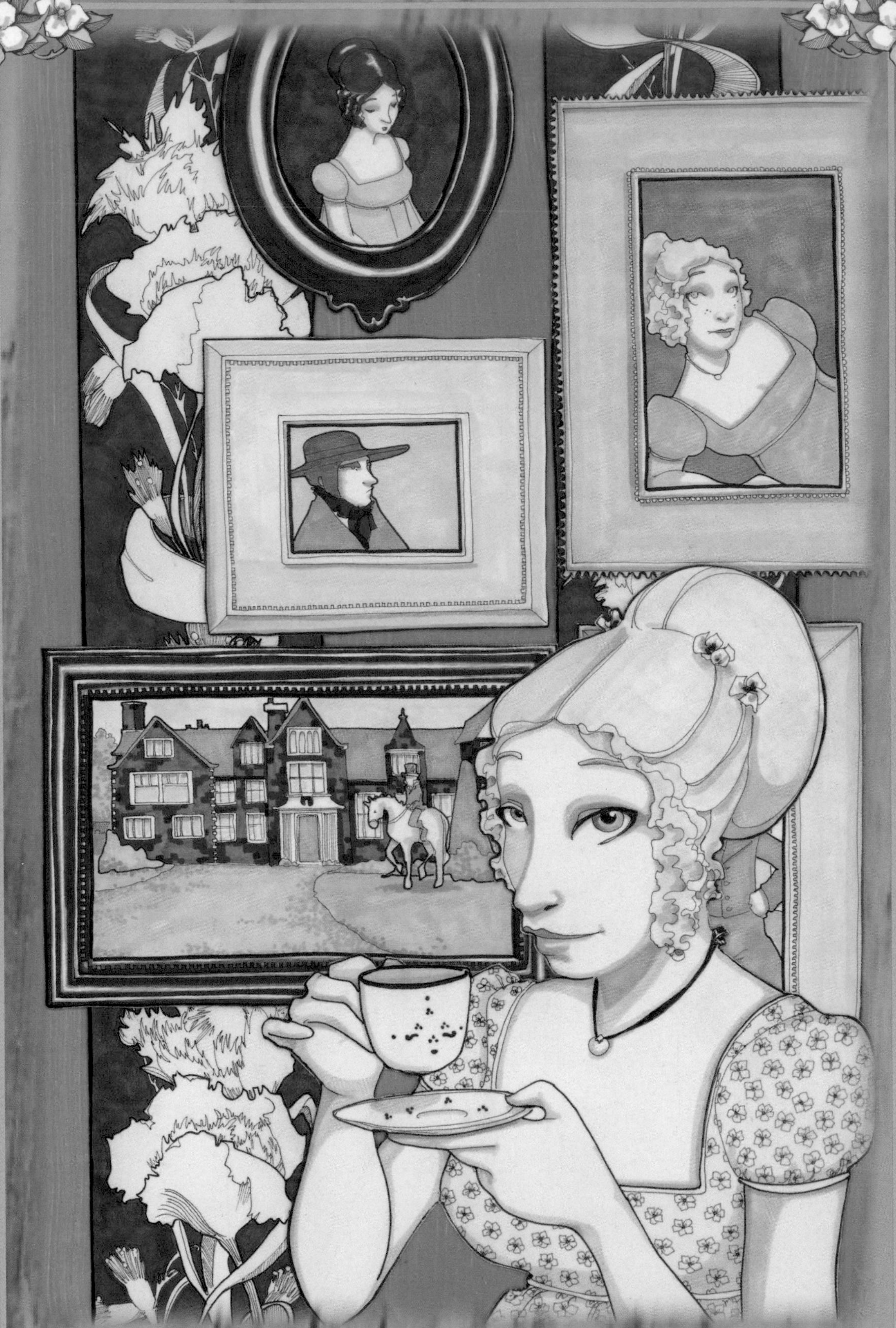

Four

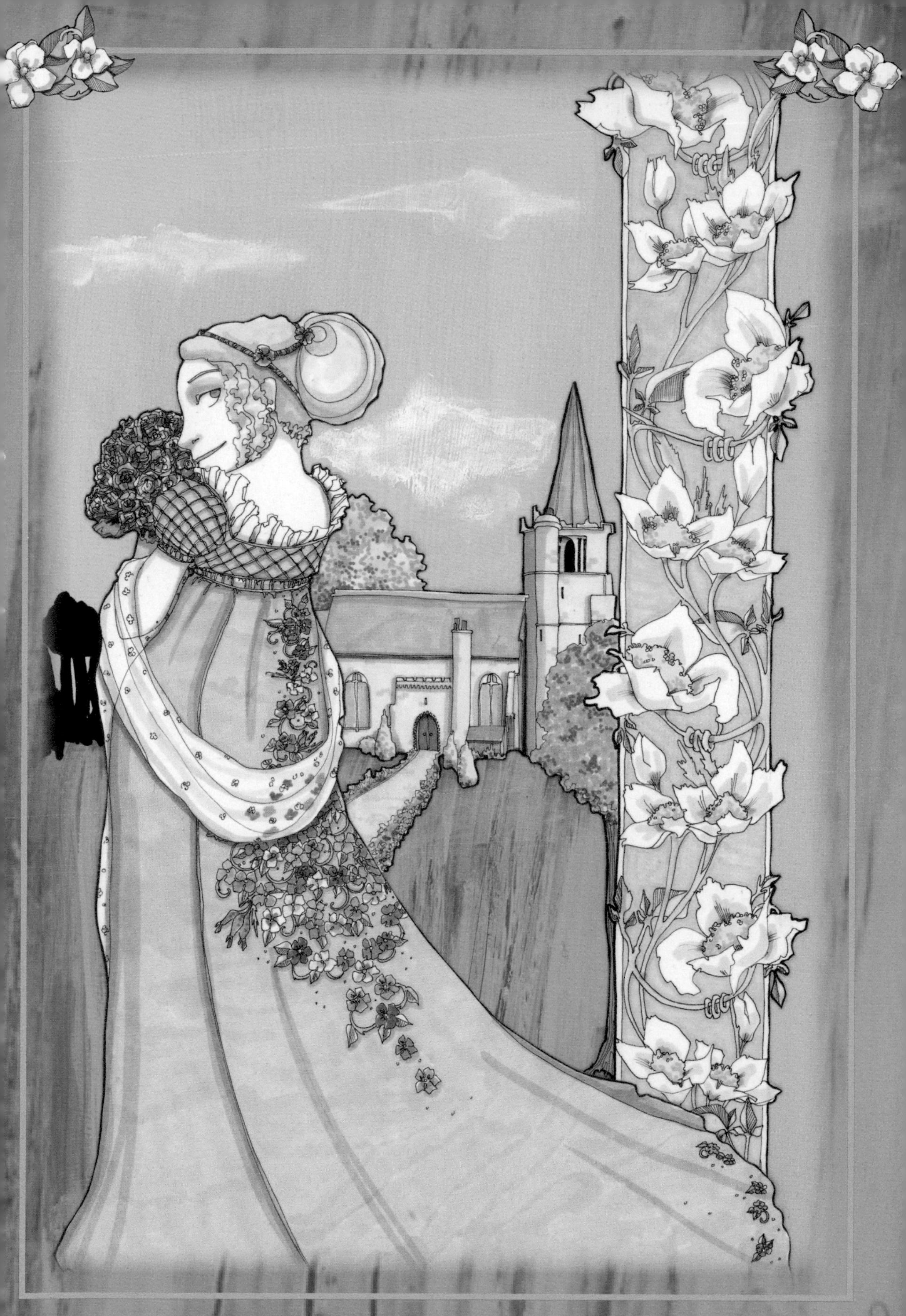

Five

Look for other
~ JANE AUSTEN ~
adaptations

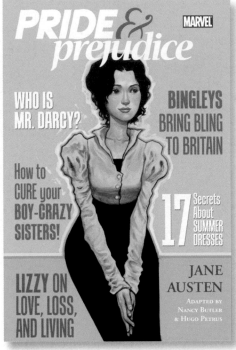

Pride & Prejudice Premiere Hardcover
Adapted by Nancy Butler & Hugo Petrus
978-0-7851-3915-7

Sense & Sensibility Premiere Hardcover
Adapted by Nancy Butler & Sonny Liew
ISBN 978-0-7851-4819-7